Praise for *Jimmy the Wags*

"Beneath the swagger and wisecracks, Wagner's embellished yarns of his post-NYPD career as a P.I. ring true. . . . An entertaining glimpse into an on-the-edge lifestyle." —*Booklist*

"As cops privately will, Wagner crudely skewers most everyone in his way: inept FBI agents, Mafia goombahs, stool pigeons and their harridan wives. Yet his capacity to note the subtle absurdities of situations both banal and dangerous elevates this above the level of mere dreary war stories . . . more than just entertainment." —*Kirkus Reviews*

"Action-packed." —*Star*

"A gritty, outrageous memoir." —*Staten Island Advance*

D0881164

Jimmy the Wags

street
stories
of a
private
eye

James Wagner,

with Patrick Picciarelli

AN ONYX BOOK

ONYX
Published by New American Library, a division of
Penguin Putnam Inc., 375 Hudson Street,
New York, New York 10014, U.S.A.
Penguin Books Ltd, 27 Wrights Lane,
London W8 5TZ, England
Penguin Books Australia Ltd, Ringwood,
Victoria, Australia
Penguin Books Canada Ltd, 10 Alcorn Avenue,
Toronto, Ontario, Canada M4V 3B2
Penguin Books (N.Z.) Ltd, 182–190 Wairau Road,
Auckland 10, New Zealand

Penguin Books Ltd, Registered Offices:
Harmondsworth, Middlesex, England

Published by Onyx, an imprint of New American Library, a division of
Penguin Putnam Inc. This is an authorized reprint of a hardcover edition
published by William Morrow and Company, Inc.
For information address William Morrow and Company, Inc.,
10 East Fifty-third Street, New York, N.Y. 10022.

First Onyx Printing, June 2000
10 9 8 7 6 5 4 3 2

For my loving wife, Pat,
who held me up when it felt like
I must have weighed a ton.
To my children who
were understanding and
told me to "go for it."
I love you.

To Don Imus: If it weren't for that quiet Sunday morning when we sat together in the kitchen at Teterboro Airport, none of this would have happened. Your encouragement gave me the final push I needed to tell my story. To ICM agents Esther Newberg, Nicole Clemens, and especially Kris Dahl: You all personify the word "professionalism." To my editor, Paul Bresnick at William Morrow: You are a class act. To Beau Dietl, who has a hard head and a soft heart: You'll live with me forever. To Tommy and Frank Piccirillo for backing me up when I needed it. And finally to Pat Picciarelli, my co-author and an incredible talent who has become a close friend: You climbed into my head and were right on the money. I could not have picked a better crew for my magic carpet ride.

A man's errors are his portals of discovery.
—*James Joyce*

prologue

After twenty-two years on The Job, I know my bad guys. I'm standing in the hallway of Queens Supreme Court playing a little game. I call it, "Guess the Jailbird." It's simple to play; you look at all the people slouching against the walls in the courthouse and try to guess who's been in jail and who's about to go to jail for the first time. An ex-con sticks out like a black person at a Klan rally. A person who's done time looks around by moving only the head, not the whole body like the average person does. More like an animal. The next time you watch the Discovery channel, watch the big cats. All predators do it. Most convicts are predators—at least those who survive.

My name is James Wagner; my friends call me Wags. I retired eight years ago with the rank of sergeant from the New York City Police Department. I now make my living as a licensed private investigator and security consultant. It gets to be second nature. I'm the kind of guy who watches boxing on television and scans the

1

crowd for lowlifes. I always considered myself very streetwise, even as a kid. If I were blind, you could put me in a room with thirty people and I'd tap the person on the shoulder who had committed a crime.

Today I'd be tapping myself on the shoulder. I'm in court on a criminal case.

My own.

I've pleaded guilty to robbery. Today I'm getting sentenced.

The robbery charge is the result of a security assignment gone bad. I'm facing time in jail and I'm scared witless. My attorney, George DiLeo, tries to reassure me.

"Relax," he says. "You're not going to jail. We'll be out of here in an hour." He adjusts the knot on his ninety-dollar tie and pinches the crease on the pants of his Brioni suit. I can't help thinking that I helped pay for his wardrobe. His fee and other legal costs have set me back twenty thousand dollars. Even though I've known George for years, this is the first time he's represented me in a criminal matter. I'm like a bridegroom about to march down the aisle. Did I make the right choice?

"I'm glad you're so confident"—I feel sweat trickle down my back—"you're not the one facing the wicked witch of the north." The lady judge I had pulled had been dour at my arraignment. I was definitely not looking forward to facing her again.

I had started the day in my home on Staten Island. My wife of twenty-three years, Pat, wanted to come to court with me but I wanted to do this alone. I'm the tough one in the family. At least I think I am. My four kids are aware that I'm in trouble but I've kept the facts to myself.

JIMMY THE WAGS

The drive to Queens seems like it takes forever. It's the first really hot day in June. Summer has hit New York City like an artillery round. Spring, it seems, lasted about an hour and a half. The humidity festival that is New York in the summer has begun.

The door to part K-21 swings open. A court officer who doesn't look old enough to shave waves us in. "You're up," he says, trying not to look smug. Some wanna-be cops get intense satisfaction from seeing a New York City cop squirm. George grabs my arm and we go inside.

The next ten minutes are a blur. My heart's pounding like a bass drum and I'm wondering if anyone can see the throbbing artery in my neck. I know I feel it. I'm light-headed. If I black out, I have every intention of grabbing my lawyer's arm and ripping the sleeve off his two-thousand-dollar suit as I hit the floor. I wonder if the judge knows that George's brother-in-law is a "made" man in a crime family. Just my luck she'll be aware of this and it will go against me.

I hear snippets of what the judge is saying.

". . . ought to be ashamed . . . community service . . . loss of PI license . . ."

The next thing I recall is my lawyer leading me out of the courtroom. He backs me up against a wall and talks without moving his lips. His eyes dart around the hallway. "See, not too bad. One hundred hours of community service and five years' probation. They took your PI ticket. Big fucking deal. Piece of cake."

My suit jacket is soaked through despite the air-conditioning. Most of the crowd has lingered, awaiting their time in the arena. Strangely, I feel a kinship, even with the cons.

I lick my lips. I want a cigarette badly. At least no jail time. "I think I should call my wife."

George looks at his watch. "Yeah, good idea." He's chewing gum. I wonder where he got it. "Listen, I hate to bring this up . . . the money?"

I start to return to reality. "Oh, yeah." I give him the balance of what I owe him, in cash. I had to get a second mortgage on my home to pay the guy. I should have been a lawyer.

I see the assistant district attorney, Dugan, the ADA who prosecuted me, come out of the courtroom. He nods and starts walking over. Now what? Dugan is a ruddy-faced Irishman in his mid-forties still hanging on to a job that the average ADA leaves five years after graduating from law school. Either he has no ambition or he has too much integrity. Pick one.

He's breathless from walking across the hall. Too many late nights in the saloons on Queens Boulevard. "Can I talk to your client?" he asks George, like I'm not there. Must be a lawyer thing.

George looks surprised by the request. "Yeah, sure, why the hell not?" He assumes a lawyer pose—brows knit together, arms folded, about to defend my rights with everything he can muster. That, and to justify the twenty big ones I gave him for what I figure to be three hours' work.

Dugan extends his hand to me. I reach out instinctively. "I want to wish you luck," he says. "I don't normally do this to someone I've just prosecuted, but the whole case was a raw deal. I was just doing my job."

I can't believe what I'm hearing. Like an idiot, I look around to see if a reporter has heard what he just said. Headline: "Wags Ain't Such a Bad Guy After All." The only thing I see is a bunch of basket cases chewing on their lips, but I am genuinely touched. If he wants absolution, he's got it from me. I repeat robotically, "Sure, I know, just doing your job. No hard feelings." He smiles crookedly, averts his eyes, and walks away.

George pats me on the back. "Wags, call me if you need me." He snaps his gum and strides down the hall. He's the last guy I hope I ever have to call.

I have to wait for a free phone. What do I want to do most—call my wife or have a cigarette? I wait for the phone. That's love. I feel a strange sense of relief. The fear of the unknown is over; at least I'm not going to jail. I may be without a livelihood, damn near broke, and a convicted felon, but at least I won't be sharing a cell with someone named Bubba for the next few years. Ex-cops don't last long in prison.

I drop a quarter and I'm beginning to punch buttons when I feel a hand on my shoulder. Instinctively, I touch my elbow to my side to feel for my gun. All I feel is a beefy hip.

"You James Wagner?" The man asking the question sticks an ID wallet in my face: "Special Agent Garay, Department of Labor." He's young, wearing the uniform of a federal agent: gray suit, rep tie, laced shoes. If I had opened up a gray-suit store outside 26 Federal Plaza when I retired instead of trying to be Indiana Jones, I wouldn't be in the fix I'm in.

I squeak out a yes. The fear that had left me ten minutes before is making an unscheduled return. My stomach tightens; I get light-headed again.

"For you." He holds papers against my chest. "You've been served." He's done his job; he turns and starts to walk away.

I grab his arm, wondering if I've just assaulted a fed-

eral officer. "What's this all about?" The words come
out like I'm chewing on a sock.

Surprisingly, he's cordial. "Carpenters' union. You
work for the carpenters' union?"

I nod absently. I'd been doing collections for them
for a few years. There had been rumors of a federal investigation. A few months back I had been interviewed by the FBI but had heard nothing since.

"There's a grand jury investigating misappropriation of union funds and labor racketeering. They
wanna talk to you."

I'm incredulous. "Me? I'm a bodyguard. I do some
minor investigations and arrears collections every
now and then. Am I a target?" There are two categories
of witnesses in a grand-jury proceeding; targets and
everyone else. I'm praying I fall into the latter cate-
gory.

Garay shrugs. "I'm only the messenger. Just show
up." He's gone.

Thoughts of calling my wife take a temporary backseat to a mental slide show of my years with the union.
The carpenters' union is typical of most labor organi-
zations; allegations of corruption are endemic. I rack
my brain to try to remember if I was privy to any criminal activity. I'm also thinking that a judge just gave
me five years' probation and within ten minutes I'm in
jeopardy of violating the conditions by getting into
trouble again.

I need a cigarette. I step outside into a blast furnace,
but I was sweating long before I hit the street. The
Lucky Strike calms me down, but only temporarily.
Twenty-two years, I think. I'd put in most of my time
in Bed-Stuy and the East Village. The armpits of New
York City. Never once in trouble. I'd received over

thirty awards and commendations as a cop, including the New York State Medal of Valor.

My legs feel rubbery. I find what passes for a clean spot on a bench outside the courthouse. How the hell did I get myself in this fix?

chapter one

I have the same view of retirement day as every other cop: We envision a grateful city bestowing kudos for a job well done, perhaps a few handshakes and back-slaps. The reality is depressing.

I have a friend who was a paratrooper in the army. After being pumped up with a lot of gung-ho propaganda during three grueling weeks of jump school, when he made his fifth and final jump, he expected a brass band to meet him on the ground. He thought the ceremony where he received his coveted jump wings would be steeped in military pomp. Instead, a buck private met him and handed him a pair of silver wings from a crumbling cardboard box. The New York City Police Department, being a quasi-military organization, obviously took a few pages from military text.

I got the bum's rush out of the pension section and had to put up with a bunch of sarcastic civilians in the license division where I went to get the obligatory carry-pistol permit. Up until a few years ago, the department made retirees pay a few hundred dollars in fees to get the permit, so I guess I was supposed to be grateful I was saving a few bucks.

The entire retirement process took a few hours. Don't let the door to 1 Police Plaza hit you in the ass on the way out. 'Bye.

Twenty-two years.

I could have done at least another ten but I finally realized that the NYPD is no place for an adult. Even with the rank of sergeant, I felt stifled. The Job encourages little independent thinking. Make a legitimate mistake and, if it's politically expedient, you get fed to the wolves. With an unblemished record, I had known it was only a matter of time until I'd have either had to take responsibility for the stupid mistake of one of my twenty-one-year-old charges or be forced to shoot a rampaging crackhead (who would be depicted in the newspapers as an "honor student").

Not for me. Despite being close to being promoted to lieutenant, I decided to pull the pin.

Okay, now I'm out—what do I do? It's a scary time, believe me. My father retired from The Job after twenty-eight years. I wonder how he adjusted. I should have asked. A cop's entire life revolves around The Job. The "us" against "them" mentality takes over in the academy. It's hard to shake. Now I was one of "them." As one of "them," I knew I was no longer in the fold. It's not a malicious thing on the part of active cops, but the nature of police work shuts cops off from outsiders. Twenty-two years or not, I'm now an outsider—get used to it.

I had no definite plans. My pension was decent, my wife worked, and if it came down to it, I could always sell my kids. (Police humor—I'll miss the laughs.) I had three children still living at home: James, thirteen; Jennifer, eleven; and Patricia, seven. A stepdaughter from my wife's first marriage, Susan, was twenty-two and lived in New Jersey. I consider her my blood. But, on with my life. I was forty-three and too young to spend the rest of my life doing nothing, or worse, spend my days making indentations on some bar with my elbows. I've seen it happen.

I took the private investigator's exam and passed. I had spent a long time acquiring contacts in the law-enforcement community and I figured a PI license would get me some work with attorneys. It was either that or become a writer. The trend is for New York cops to want to be writers and LA cops to want to be actors. I wonder what Chicago cops want to be. Unindicted? The PI ticket seemed the logical way to go. I'd always been street-smart, and I had a flair for thinking on my feet, attributes I thought necessary in investigations and security work. Of course, a shrink would tell me that I have a craving for action, which, I guess, wouldn't be far from the truth. I remember that when I was a kid I would taunt a local candy-store owner on the way home from school. The guy hated kids, so he deserved my harassment. He was pretty quick, however, and he would chase me out of his store, sometimes with a sawed-off pool cue in his hand. I'd let him stay a few feet behind me—almost getting caught but a breath away from being brained with the pool cue. I liked the danger aspect of it. I still thirst for it.

I put out the word: The Wags was for hire. I sat by the phone. My ass didn't exactly develop calluses, but it had come close by the time the phone finally rang.

* * *

It was Beau Dietl, ace private eye (his own description).

I had known Beau from the PD. He'd been a hot shot detective who'd retired on disability when he'd injured himself in a skydiving accident. He'd been guarding some Middle Eastern types on his off-duty time. They'd wanted to go skydiving and Beau had gone along. He had never jumped before but the Arabs had been paratroopers in their country and knew what they were doing.

Beau is a character. He loves publicity. His office walls are crammed with pictures of him with anyone he can find wearing a tuxedo. One of his greatest loves is gangsters. I'm convinced that in a former life he was Al Capone. He hangs around gangsters, dresses like them, walks the walk and talks the talk.

One couldn't deny that he was successful, however. In the seven years he'd been out of The Job, he'd built a thriving business. He gave me my first assignment.

I had gone to his office because he didn't want to discuss business over the phone. Most cops have a natural distaste for telephones. We always think they're tapped.

"Wanna guard some Arabs?" Right to the point. Beau was behind an aircraft-carrier-size desk. He's a compact guy, around five-eight and built like a bull. He likes big things: cars, cigars, women.

I'd never done bodyguard work before and I told him so.

"What's to know? I'll put you with two other retired guys who do this stuff for me all the time." Beau gave me the details. Six Arab princes from the Saudi royal family were flying in from Las Vegas. They didn't rate State Department protection, too low-level. New York

12

was sort of a last-minute idea, rather than going straight home. They had called Beau for security. They were staying at the Waldorf Towers and wanted bodyguards who knew the city.

"I'll give you three hundred fifty a day, plus expenses. They'll probably be in town about a week."

I did some quick mental math. I'd clear more in three days with Beau than I'd taken home in two weeks from the police department. "Anything I need to know?" Police-speak for "Give me the downside."

Beau smiled. "Nothing, other than I'm doing you a favor." He leaned over his desk to give me the once-over. "Got better clothes?"

I felt self-conscious and instinctively ran a hand down the sleeve of my JCPenney special. I was never much of a clotheshorse and I was wearing the only suit I owned. My family couldn't eat a Versace suit. "No good?"

He shrugged. "By the time this job is over, you'll be shopping at Barneys." He tossed me a folded index card and a copy of Zagat's restaurant guide. "You're going to need the book. Be at the address on the card tomorrow morning at eight."

At home that night I reviewed in my mind what little I knew about Saudi Arabia. All citizens were Muslims, of this much I was certain. That meant they didn't smoke, drink, do drugs, or fool around with women. I was probably in for a boring week, but at $350 a day, who cared?

I met up with the other two retired detectives the next morning in a Queens diner not too far from the JFK airport. They were dressed like bankers—and I'm not talking tellers. Their shoes alone must have cost more than my wife's wedding dress. They introduced themselves and seemed friendly. Frank was the older of the two, probably around fifty, in good shape and around six feet two; Tony was about forty-five, a hair shorter and swarthy. Frank's face rang no bells, but Tony looked very familiar. I would find out later that he'd formerly been with the Special Investigation Unit (SIU), a corrupt branch of the police department on which the movie *Prince of the City* was based. During my assignment with the Arabs, I found out that he'd done time in prison for his involvement in organized-crime activity. Today I hear he's an actor and has appeared in *GoodFellas*, among other pictures. That morning we relaxed over breakfast and I was advised of the drill.

"We're basically social directors," Frank said. "They tell us where they want to go and what they want to do and we make the arrangements."

"There's no threat?"

Both men laughed. "You may get a hernia lifting suitcases full of money, but that's about it," Tony said. I was told that they carried at least two million in cash with them.

"What for?" I asked. "I thought these guys spent their time praying to Mecca."

Frank and Tony exchanged glances. Frank said, "Where they live, they don't drink, smoke, or have any vices—"

"Until their feet hit the tarmac at Kennedy," Tony interjected, "then it's 'give me booze, give me drugs, give me broads.'"

I tried not to act surprised, but a mental picture of the Ayatollah smoking a joint sprang to mind. It seemed ludicrous.

Our charges came in on a commercial jet. There were

six princes, dressed in casual Western attire. They introduced themselves, all speaking in broken English. Smiles and handshakes all around. They seemed to be in their mid-thirties, except for a seventh man, younger than the others, carrying an attaché case, and standing in the background. He didn't speak at all for the entire limo ride into Manhattan and I was later told that he spoke little if any English and was basically a flunkie, or glorified servant. Frank and Tony called him Dickhead because he didn't know what they were saying. They would yell out "Dickhead!" when they needed something and he would smile benignly. The attaché case he was carrying contained a little over two million in cash. Party money, I was told.

The suite at the Waldorf Towers was elegant. We each had our own rooms. It took our royalty over an hour to unpack the thirty-odd suitcases they had with them. Within two hours we were shopping in stores along Fifth Avenue. They paid cash for everything; Dickhead kept doling out the money. The attaché case lid was opening and closing like an alligator's jaws. And what do you think they bought? More suitcases. In fact, they kept on buying suitcases for the entire seven days we were with them. They didn't buy clothes to put in them, just empty suitcases. This idiosyncrasy was the first of several I encountered.

A little after returning to the suite, one of the princes approached me and asked that I make reservations in a good French restaurant. I whipped out Zagat's, to be guided by the ratings. I felt a hand on my shoulder. It was Tony.

"What are you doing?"

I told him. He shook his head.

"I'll do it. I know what they want. Put the book away." He smiled.

We went to a very expensive restaurant on Fifty-seventh Street. I'd have to mortgage my house—again—to afford a meal there. Frank and Tony were greeted like long-lost relatives by the owner. Hugs and cheek kisses. I hadn't gotten that much affection from my parents when I'd gotten back from the navy. Something was up. There were people waiting at the bar for tables. We were taken care of immediately. The princes sat down and we got a table to ourselves. It was then that I was introduced to idiosyncrasy number two. They started with dessert and worked backward! They were like kids in a candy store. They ate at least ten different desserts and then started on the entrées. Tony told me they didn't eat sweets where they lived and pigged out on anything that contained sugar when they came to America.

The way they drank, you would have thought Prohibition was starting the next day. I stopped counting after eight bottles of Dom Pérignon. They ordered thirty-year-old single-malt scotch as chasers. They didn't care if we drank, but there was no way we could keep up with them. We ate well and drank plenty. Our guard was definitely down. If a team of assassins had come into the restaurant at the end of the four-hour dinner, they could have wiped us out and the sounds of gunfire would have been muffled by the burps, belches, and farts. That was them, not us. I served with a better class of Appalachian white trash in the navy.

The check came to over four thousand dollars. No problem. Dickhead paid cash and tipped generously.

While Tony huddled with the owner, Frank and I

poured Saudi Arabia's leadership into the limo. They went to their respective rooms at the hotel and passed out. I was about to do the same when Tony handed me an envelope.

"What's this?"

"Your cut."

"Cut from what?"

"This is why we pick the restaurants, Wags. We get a percentage of the check for steering them to places that take care of us." There was two hundred dollars in the envelope. Welcome to the free-enterprise system. Initially, I felt a little guilty about taking the money, but I had to remind myself that I wasn't on The Job anymore. I wasn't breaking any laws. After a week of lunches and dinners, I'd make an extra fifteen hundred dollars. And that was only the beginning.

The next morning—late morning—we shopped again. This time we got as far as a furrier in the Waldorf lobby and one of the princes bought a mink coat. I doubt it was for his wife unless they were going to attach a full-head hood and cut out eye holes. The coat cost twenty grand. Now, I realize that these guys were extravagant, but a mink in one of those hotel stores probably costs at least twice what it would cost in the garment district, which was a ten-minute limo ride away. I started to say something and Frank read my mind. He shook his head. I smelled another finder's fee. The system wasn't too hard to figure out. I backed off. We split three thousand dollars.

We hit more stores. One men's apparel place on the east side actually shut down the store so we could have privacy. The Saudis didn't go in there for clothes, though; you guessed it—more suitcases. We had to get another limo just to lug the suitcases back to the hotel.

There was a conference back at the suite. The princes spoke Arabic among themselves, then one of them approached me. Frank and Tony were nowhere to be found. It was the same one who'd asked me to make the dinner reservation. I guessed he was the mouthpiece.

"Women," he said.

"Yeah," I replied. "What about them?"

"You can get us women?"

Show me a New York City cop who can't get a prostitute on short notice and I'll show you a fireman. "No problem. Six, right?"

"No, seven."

I guess they were going to take care of Dickhead. They wanted the girls back in the room at nine o'clock. That gave us about three hours. I could round up the Dallas Cowboys' cheerleaders by then. "Not a problem." Frank and Tony reappeared. "We've got a chore," I said. "Girls. Back here by nine."

"Seven, right?" Tony said.

I was puzzled. How'd they know the princes were going to be benevolent and take care of their servant? "How'd you—"

Frank said, "We've done this a lot of times. No matter how many in the party, they always ask for an additional girl. They discard one."

I had visions of a hooker flying out the window. "Discard?"

"Not what you're thinking. In this case they'll pick six, pay the seventh but tell her to walk. Don't ask, I haven't got a clue." Dickhead was going to have to rely on a jar of Vaseline and a copy of *Penthouse*.

I was informed by Frank that the girls had better be first-class. It turned out that it was a lot more difficult to get seven quality hookers assembled in three hours than I'd thought it would be. Finally, after working three phones we'd compiled our own little harem. I volunteered to go down to the lobby and check them out.

Drop-dead gorgeous, each one of them. They must have gone into collective bargaining while they waited because they all charged the same fee. Two hundred and fifty dollars an hour. Up front. I didn't want to commit our clients' money without getting the okay, so I left the blushing virgins in the lobby and went back upstairs to get a green light.

Prince Mouthpiece was incensed.

"Two hundred and fifty dollars!"

These were the last guys I wanted to piss off. I was already thinking private schools for my kids. "Too much?"

"Too much? Not enough! We want five-hundred-an-hour girls." He looked at his watch. "And we want them in an hour. We want to go to clubs. Get them out of the hotel and get us better girls. Now!" He turned his back and strode away. The Prince of Chides, touchy when he was horny. I was dismissed. Dickhead appeared from out of nowhere and gave me ten thousand dollars in hundred-dollar bills. This called for a conference. It took Frank, Tony, and myself thirty seconds to come up with a solution.

I went back to the lobby with the cash. "Let's go, ladies," I said, "in the limo." Every male head in the lobby was turned in our direction as we left. In the car I gave the girls what they'd asked for—two hundred and fifty an hour each for two hours plus a hundred-dollar tip to say they were charging five hundred an hour. The driver got fifty. The rest belonged to the fearless bodyguards. We drove around the East Side for a while, drank three bottles of Dom Pérignon, and got back to the hotel in exactly an hour.

The princes were happy and I was now a master of the system, not to mention a pimp.

At midnight I was ready for bed and I figured the Saudis would be too. After the girls left, however, they were as good as their word. Party time.

Dressed like six John Travolta clones they were primed and ready to go. Polyester permeated the room. We figured that if there was going to be any trouble, it would happen in the clubs. You never know who you might offend in a New York City nightspot. It was late; wanna-be wiseguys ruled Midtown. Most carried guns, all had knives. Look at the wrong girl and it could be O.K. Corral time. Hell, this was what we were getting paid for. I'm a little over six feet tall and I had practiced my scowl for twenty-two years to intimidate prisoners. Frank and Tony looked like part of Murder, Inc. We could handle whatever came along.

Our first stop was Club A in the shadow of the Queensboro Bridge. Six years ago, when we went there, it was a happening place. It must have been packed. A line was queued around the block. Tony got Dickhead's attention.

"Case," Tony said. The money-bearer knew that much English. He popped it open and looked at his bosses.

Mouthpiece said, "Tip everyone one hundred dollars. Get us in."

Frank took a wad of bills from Dickhead. "Wait in the car." He vanished under an awning and was back in minutes. "Took care of all four bouncers and the doorman." He held out what remained of the money to Dickhead.

Mouthpiece waved an arm. "Hold on to it. This is just the first stop."

The place was a wall-to-wall party. There was no way we could protect these guys if they decided to mingle. To my surprise they got a table—another hundred to a waiter—and just observed. They sat there for three hours and watched people boogie. Go figure. We stood by the bar and ran up a two-hundred-dollar tab. I was on my fourth drink when Tony jammed some bills in my pocket. It was hard to believe, but money was beginning to bore me.

"And what's this for, not taking a piss in the last twenty minutes?" I fingered three hundred-dollar bills.

"Me and Frank figure we don't want to spoil the help. A Benjie is a bit much to tip these guys. I switched the hundreds for twenties. They're happy with twenty, we split eighty." He smiled, pleased with himself. Sounded about right to me.

We hit two more clubs on the east side. The Saudis repeated the act, sitting at a table and consuming copious amounts of liquor. When we hit the third place, the three of us nursed one drink each. I hadn't drunk this much since my bachelor party. My head was spinning. I looked at my watch: 3:00 A.M. I staggered over to the princes' table. Believe it or not, they looked sober.

"Bars in New York close in thirty minutes; we should start wrapping it up." I stretched the truth by thirty minutes; they close at four, but my two new best friends and I wanted to get back to the hotel. Six heads huddled together. Another furious discussion in Arabic.

The spokesman wiggled a finger. I leaned over the table. "Wags, could we have some coke?"

I felt like saying, "You can have a gallon of Diet-fucking-Pepsi if you want, just drink up and let's get the hell out of here." Instead, I found the waitress and ordered the sodas.

When the drinks arrived, I got six—seven, if you counted Dickhead—blank stares. "No, Wags," the prince said, "coke." He shoved a finger up his nose. Very subtle. Great, now we're drug dealers. I wanted no part of it but I nodded and went back to the bar.

I related our clients' wishes to Tony and Frank.

"To tell you the truth," Frank said above the din, "I'm surprised they waited this long to ask us. Let me make a call."

I grabbed his arm. "You mean you're gonna make a drug sale?" I suddenly felt sober.

"Wags, lemme explain something to you"—he put an arm around my shoulders—"we don't do this and the next time these guys come in they ask for someone else to protect them. If it's not them, it'll be some other Arabs. The word'll get around if we don't do the right thing. *Capeesh?* We ain't cops anymore. These are our clients, we're not selling the shit on the street." He looked around the bar to make sure no one was listening. "You'll get stranger requests than this if you stay in this business." How true those words were, I was to find out.

A moral dilemma. I balk and I ruin it for the two guys I'm working with. I go along with it and I'm a criminal. Frank and Tony saw me struggling.

"I'll tell you what, Wags, sit this one out. Me'n Frank'll take care of it." Tony nodded reassuringly. I felt relieved. Tony was gone for no more than twenty minutes. He gestured from the doorway when he got back. I gathered up the party animals and we piled into the limo.

There was still plenty of room in the superstretch even with nine of us in the back. Dickhead rode with the driver. The glass privacy panel slid up for the first time that night. Tony tossed a baggieful of white powder to one of the princes. Smiles and giggles. These guys were going to be hurting tomorrow.

Lines were laid out as thick as cigars on a fold-out table. They bumped heads trying to be the first to get at them. By the time we got back to the hotel, they'd gone through about five grams. The party continued in the suite. I tried to get some sleep, but it was impossible. Our diplomats—they had diplomatic immunity as members of the royal family—talked an insane gibberish until noon. They finally collapsed in the living room and I got Frank and Tony to help me carry them to their rooms.

I had assumed money was made on the drug deal, but I didn't get any. I wanted it that way. That night while the Saudis lay comatose, Frank, Tony, and I got out for a little while to have a quiet dinner in a restaurant near the hotel. Tony began to talk about ripping off Dickhead for what remained of the money he was carrying around in the attaché case. He said he was only fantasizing and Frank jumped right in. They figured they could have a confederate slug him when he went to the john in one of the clubs. The whole thing would take less than a minute. What did I think?

"You're kidding, right?" I said.

Tony and Frank exchanged glances. "Yeah, sure," Frank said, "but do you think it could be done?" He had an intense look in his eyes, like he was studying my reaction to the plan.

I wasn't sure whether it was just a fantasy. "One of us is supposed to go to the can with him," I said warily. Why didn't I think this was a game?

"We've missed trips to the bathroom before, this could be one of those times. Waddaya think?" Tony said.

I laughed. "I think from now on one of us should go to the bathroom with him." They weren't amused, but there was no further discussion about their little "fantasy." The security business, I was discovering, wasn't inhabited by saints.

We had a reprieve the next day—the boys were strung out—but we resumed at full tilt the following day. More women, drugs, and booze. We hit a different expensive restaurant for both lunch and dinner. By the end of the week, I had gained seven pounds. Dickhead slipped me an envelope at the airport before the princes boarded the plane to go home. Another three grand, split among us. With my salary, I cleared close to five thousand dollars. Frank and Tony wanted to celebrate after the Saudis departed but all I wanted to do was go home.

My family was glad to see me and I was happy to be home. We paid a major portion of our bills early that month and I was able to buy two suits, which I figured I would need in the business world. I went to Barneys, where else?

chapter two

The word was getting around: Hire The Wags and be assured he would show up for whatever job was available. After the Arabs, the phone never stopped ringing. I've got to thank Beau Dietl for most of the work I got initially, but after a while I started to build my own client base.

I was making more money than I'd ever imagined. My original fantasy about sending my kids to private schools was becoming a reality faster than I'd expected. The more diverse my clients, the more I knew that a good wardrobe was essential. I began to appreciate fine clothes within two months of getting into my new business. My one extravagance was a weekly manicure. Good clothes were necessary to blend in with corporate clients; a manicure was a luxury. To this day I still get a weekly manicure.

One of my first celebrity clients was John Walsh from *America's Most Wanted*. He received many death threats from the criminals he helped put away as well as the garden-variety nuts who thought they were John Gotti. Mr. Walsh was a gentleman with a heavy burden to bear. His son, Adam, was brutally murdered in Florida, a crime that is still unsolved. He was obsessed with catching bad guys, and I enjoyed the four months I spent with him shuttling back and forth between New York and Washington, D.C., where the television studio was located. It was an easy gig. Other than a few threatening phone calls and letters, I never had to confront a stalker or jump in front of a bullet.

The show was supposedly live but was actually taped. The sea of people TV viewers saw on their sets purportedly answering phones were actors. Six hours later when the show aired and viewers called in with tips, a few guys in jeans and T-shirts answered the phones in a cluttered studio office.

I also guarded major stars. One night I had Robert DeNiro and Martin Scorsese. They kept mostly to themselves but were nice guys, very friendly. Halfway through the night I got the urge to do an imitation of DeNiro doing the "Mook" dialogue from *Mean Streets*. Actually, it was a toss-up between that and the "Are you looking at me?" monologue from *Taxi Driver*. The retired cop I was working with was mortified when I brought it up. He told me he would personally shoot me if I tried it. I was all set to launch into my act in an elevator when I saw my partner's hand on his gun. Some people have no sense of humor.

As interesting as these jobs were, I was bored. I was thirsting for excitement. I'm a "thrill of the kill" kind of person. My best friends in those days were Jerome X. O'Donovan, Eddie Soper, and Walter Rannow. Jerome is a New York City councilman today, Eddie was killed in Vietnam, and Walter committed suicide by jumping in front of a train.

We used to go to the top of the Verrazano-Narrows Bridge, which connects Staten Island to Brooklyn. At the time, it was under construction. We would take the catwalk to the highest tower and dare each other to stand on a parapet and "hang ten." For those unfamiliar with the surfing term, that means we would stand on a tower with our toes hanging over the edge. We were hundreds of feet straight up! We would do this for hours. Of course, a couple of six-packs helped fuel our bravado. I still get a rush thinking about it. Walter, by the way, jumped in front of that train on a dare after a night of partying in the old Electric Circus in the East Village. It was the final rush for him.

I was close to expiring from terminal boredom when Beau Dietl came to the rescue, asking me to meet him in his office the following day. In attendance were five retired detectives.

"What I got here," Beau said, "is a custodial interference job." He passed out pictures of a woman about thirty years old and an eighteen-month-old boy. "Daddy's our client. He got a divorce from the lady in the picture and got custody of the kid." He went on to tell us that the ex-wife was from Denmark. "The ex took the kid for a weekend six months ago and flew to Denmark with him. She ain't coming back."

There was an instant consternation in the office. All the guys were cursing and vowing to get the kid back to Daddy. You could feel a river of testosterone coursing through the room. Cops, you see, are very vocal when it comes to protecting the rights of children. Most of us come from large middle-class families and have numerous children ourselves. Over the years we've seen too many abused and mistreated kids to take it lightly.

"I'm glad you guys all wanna get involved. First, there ain't much money in it. Daddy's not all that well-heeled. Second, we gotta go to Denmark and kidnap the kid." Now everybody shut up. Convictions are one thing, money's another, and getting locked up in Denmark is still another. I could read the expressions on their faces: Hey, the kid'll learn to love Mommy.

Beau feigned confusion. "What, no volunteers?" He went around the room. Everyone had an excuse. One guy said his grandmother had just died. (I'd gone to her funeral two years before.) All the other excuses were just as lame.

I raised a finger. "I'll go, Beau." I have to admit that my volunteering wasn't all that altruistic. Sure, I felt for the little boy, but mainly I needed a little excitement in my life.

Beau looked around the room. "That's me and The Wags. Who else?" No one uttered a peep. "Okay, you supercops, class dismissed." The five heroes shuffled out. Beau gave me more particulars.

"The wife, Charlotte, has dual citizenship, Danish and American. The little boy has an American passport. Jerry—our client—and Charlotte were married in Illinois. Jerry's an American. She travels frequently to Denmark to see her parents. That's where she is now."

"Where in Denmark?" I asked, not that I knew Denmark from New Jersey, it was just that I felt the need to hold up my end of the conversation.

Beau shuffled through a file. "Viborg." He spelled it. "Her parents own a farm a few miles outside town. They also have some kind of business there." The father, Beau said, had been trying, for six months, through the United States embassy in Copenhagen to get the kid back. He was running into a sea of red tape and uncaring diplomats. He was finally told by embassy officials that even though the boy had been born in America, once his feet hit Danish soil he was considered a Danish citizen because Mom was Danish. "We've got thirty thousand dollars to work with." To Beau, I guess that wasn't much money.

"I could put a team together."

Beau snorted. "Apparently you're going to have to. My guys fight a good battle over a bottle of Chianti in Rao's, but, as you can see, they ain't having none of this."

I ignored the comment. I might have to work with some of these guys in the future. Bad-mouth them now and word might get around. "What do we know about the layout of the house?"

"It's not gonna be easy. The father's been there before. He faxed me a map." Beau unfolded on his desk a crudely drawn map. "The farm's in the middle of nowhere. That's the good news. The bad news is that it's a long way from the airport. I figure we snatch the kid inside the house and beat feet for the airport. We could get stopped anywhere on the road if the grandparents or Mom get to a phone."

We batted this around for a while. The less time we spent on the road with the kid the better. We decided two things: One, Daddy would have to come with us just in case we got in a jam with the local authorities, and two, we needed a helicopter. I told Beau that, besides us, we would need two more experienced people on the ground.

"Well, I've got one," he said. "A girl named Sylvia.

Ex-army. Fought in the Gulf War. I've used her on a few surveillances. We could use a female for the kid. It looks better when we fly the kid home on a commercial plane."

I was skeptical. Following a cheating husband around is one thing, kidnapping is another. "You're sure she can be relied on in a tight situation? The shit hits the fan, we've gotta think fast on our feet." I didn't want to spend my next few birthdays in a Danish prison. "She's not gonna choke?"

"She can shoot Iraqis, she can do this."

He made sense, but the decision to use Sylvia would come back to haunt me.

It took me a few days but I found the other member of our team. For the purposes of this book, I'll call him Hondo.

Hondo was a former U.S. Army Ranger. I had worked with him a few months back and he was exactly what we needed: fearless and broke. My only reservation in bringing him in was that he wasn't the most mentally stable person I've worked with. One time we had a two-car surveillance going on the FDR Drive in Manhattan and to get the attention of the other car in our team he fired shots at it. He stopped after I suggested he use the cell phone. His method of reaching out and touching someone was a little strange.

He also liked good clothes. In fact, he spent all his money on Armani suits. One night he and I were coming out of a restaurant in Midtown and I happened to mention that I liked his suit.

"This fucking thing?" he said, and promptly grabbed the sleeve and ripped it from the jacket. The suit must have cost two thousand dollars. Even he realized he looked a little odd, so he ripped off the other sleeve. Now he had the only Armani vest I'd ever seen. He wore it like that the rest of the night.

We assembled our Impossible Mission Force in Beau's office a few days later. Sylvia turned out to be built like a fireplug and looked like she could handle herself. Hondo looked like Hondo, six feet four inches of potential trouble.

We mapped out a plan. We decided to base our operation in Denmark, but once we snatched the kid we would fly to Germany, about an hour's ride by chopper. We didn't want to get arrested at a Danish roadblock or sitting in a Danish airport. We would charter the helicopter under the guise of being a film crew scouting locations for a movie.

"Hondo," Beau said, "you're the advance man. Go to Denmark tomorrow"—he slid plane tickets across his desk—"and scout the farmhouse. We wanna know the comings and goings, who's going where and what time. I'll give you three days for that; report back to Wags." Hondo, it turned out, hid in a cow pasture for the entire time, sleeping next to a pile of cow shit. I'm sure that if Armani makes fatigues, Hondo wore them. He later told us that the grandparents left the house every morning at nine to drive thirty minutes to a store they owned in Viborg. They didn't return until six o'clock. This left Charlotte alone with the little boy. The plan was simple: Sylvia and I would knock on the door, push our way into the house, restrain Charlotte, and grab the kid. The father, Jerry, and Hondo would stay out of sight in case we needed them. Beau would command the operation from the helicopter, which would be hovering over a nearby field. "No need for me to be on the ground," he said, "the general never gets captured." Words to live by. The car would rendezvous with the helicopter, then we'd fly to Germany. We planned on reporting the rental car as stolen.

We had everything timed to the minute. The chopper would take us to the airport in Hamburg where we would have fifteen minutes to board a commercial flight to JFK. Piece of cake. The best-laid plans . . .

Our entourage left for Denmark the day after receiving the recon report from Hondo. We went directly to a local private airport where the helicopter and pilot awaited.

From the start, the pilot seemed suspicious. Speaking excellent English, he told us he had trained to fly in Norfolk, Virginia. We had to watch what we said around him and appear to be knowledgeable about the movie business. Collectively, we knew very little. Beau had appeared in several movies as an extra, but the extent of his expertise consisted of how to get an extra drink out of the caterers. We winged it. Most cops are good actors. We made several passes over the farmhouse. It was isolated, with one access road. The countryside was flat, with very few trees. If someone knocked me out and I woke up there, I would think I was in Kansas. The closest town was Skels, and it was about ten miles away. We didn't anticipate any problems.

After the reconnaissance flight, we checked into a motel halfway between Viborg and Skels. The team gathered at the hotel for a strategy meeting. We decided to strike the next day. I had butterflies in my stomach once the decision to go was made but I was looking forward to the thrill of the caper. Hondo was so ready he was salivating. Beau wanted to get it over with. Sylvia, on the other hand, was getting cold feet.

"What happens if we get caught?" she asked, her voice cracking.

Beau was incredulous. "We go to fucking jail, what else?" I could sense she wanted to back out.

"Look," I said, "you signed on to this job . . . you're going."

"Well, gee, I don't know. So many things could happen—"

"Yeah, one of them is you may slip and fall out of the helicopter." I was getting pissed. "I didn't come all the way to Europe to have you wimp out." I thought a moment. "What's the problem, you afraid of the Danish cops? You fought the goddamn Iraqis for Christ's sake!"

"Well, I didn't exactly fight them . . . in fact, I never even saw them." She looked at her feet and mumbled something.

Beau said, "Speak up!"

"I said, I was in communications—I strung telephone line."

Great. I gave Beau a "you asshole" look. He had recommended her but couldn't force her to break international law. Through all this, Hondo never said a thing. He just sat there in his movie-producer disguise: Gucci loafers and enough gold chains around his neck to anchor the *Queen Mary*.

Beau got up and paced the room. "Jesus fucking Christ!"

Hondo finally put his two cents in. "Sylvia," he said, quietly. "You're going." His eyes bored into hers like diamond drill bits. This is a guy who once broke another guy's arm in an elevator for accidentally pushing the wrong floor button. I guess you would say he has a low tolerance for incompetence.

I tried to be the voice of reason. "We need you, Sylvia. A kid on a plane with four guys might attract attention and we need you at the house so Charlotte doesn't get suspicious." She reluctantly agreed to go. I telephoned Jerry's room with the cryptic message, "It's a go for tomorrow."

I didn't sleep well that night; in fact, I didn't sleep at all. I was wound tighter than a spring and wanted to get the job over with. Despite my bravado, I was a little scared. I thought about not seeing my family for a few years while I languished in prison and it frightened the hell out of me. Then I thought about our client. Jerry constantly teared up when he talked about his son. Whatever his wife did to lose custody we never found out; Jerry was too much of a gentleman to mention it. I knew what I would feel like if I lost any of my kids. I couldn't wait to reunite Jerry and his son.

Morning came quickly. It was sunny and warm, a typical June day in that part of the world. Jerry was dressed casually. He was a slight man, no taller than five-five. Since he'd hired us he appeared to have lost about ten pounds. I wore a blue business suit, Sylvia was in a dress. Hondo was draped in Armani, his usual uniform. He also carried a bedsheet and an orange traffic cone. We would lay these out in a field about a mile from the farmhouse so "The General" would know where to land the chopper.

The plan was simple: Sylvia and I would identify ourselves as U.S. embassy officials with some papers for Charlotte from her ex-husband. Once she opened the door, we would force our way in. Sylvia was visibly nervous. I detected a distinct tremble in her hands. "You okay?" I asked her.

"Let's get this over with." She sounded like she'd swallowed a sweater.

It was seven A.M. The grandparents didn't leave the house until nine. We had plenty of time, so we decided to go to the airport where the chopper was and wait. When we got to the airport, we encountered our first problem.

The helicopter pilot started asking questions about the movie business and why we had to scout locations so early in the morning. He clearly didn't believe us. I looked at my watch. We had to be on the road in an hour, Beau had to be in the air in ninety minutes. The more time we spent lying to this pilot the less likely it would be that we would be going anywhere.

"Excuse me," I said to the pilot, "me and my director have to talk." I grabbed Beau by the arm and we found a quiet spot. "How much money we got?"

Beau pulled out a wad of German marks from one pocket and an equal amount in Danish currency from the other. "I dunno, maybe five large in this Kraut shit and three in the Danish money."

"I think we should give the pilot the five thousand." When all else fails, try bribery. Voted on and passed. The pilot's eyes bulged when he saw the money.

"We need you on the ground, probably on someone else's property, for maybe two minutes. You got a problem with that?" Beau asked.

The pilot was holding the money with both hands. "Someone else's property? I don't know, I could get into serious trouble . . . the police . . ."

I made a grab for the money. He pulled back, the cash still in a death grip. "Did you say two minutes? No, I don't see a problem . . . but no longer." He still had no idea why he was landing but he was willing to do it, no questions asked.

We had numerous cups of coffee. I didn't let Sky King out of my sight for a minute. I felt that given the opportunity he'd bolt with our five grand.

"Mount up!" Beau bellowed. It was 8:50.

We rode in silence. Hondo drove with me in the front seat and Sylvia was in the back. Jerry was on the floor next to her. At 9:25 we turned onto a private dirt road.

"This is the road leads to the house," Hondo said. We came into a clearing. A two-story farmhouse stood in the distance. I could make out two cars in the driveway. When we got closer, Hondo said, "We got a problem." He started to slow down.

I looked at him. "Don't slow down, keep on moving! What problem?"

"See that Volvo? It belongs to the grandparents. They haven't left yet."

From the back: "Oh shit!" It was Sylvia and Jerry in unison.

I looked at my watch. Were we too early? "Aren't they supposed to be out of here by now?"

I witnessed a first. Hondo licked his lips. He was nervous. We were less than a quarter of a mile from the house. "They leave every morning at the stroke of nine. You could set your watch by them."

We found out later that the day we'd chosen to grab the little boy was a national holiday in Denmark. Businesses were closed. I had to make a decision. Beau was somewhere above us; we heard the chopper in the distance. We had portable radios but there was no time for a conference. We had to be at the Hamburg airport in less than two hours. It was now or never. I thought about my kids. "We go!" As we passed a garage, Hondo stopped. As per our plan, he and Jerry jumped out of the car and hid. I slid into the driver's seat. Sylvia and I were on our own.

We pulled up to the house. I got out of the car with rubbery legs and a quivering gut. I glanced at Sylvia, who was pulling at her skirt to hide her nervousness. Out of the side of my mouth I said, "I'll do all the talking."

I rang the bell and waited. Within seconds an elderly woman opened the door.

"Good morning, madam," I said, smiling weakly. "My name is Robert Sanders. I'm from the American embassy." I didn't introduce Sylvia, whose heart I could swear I heard pounding. Or was it mine? "I'm sorry to disturb you so early in the morning, but we have some papers to serve on your daughter concerning her child-custody dispute with her ex-husband." I had come equipped with a small briefcase. "If we could see your daughter for a few minutes, we'll be out of here as fast as possible."

Granny agreed to get Charlotte. She left us outside and closed the door behind her. The thirty-second wait seemed like hours. Charlotte came to the door dressed in a pink bathrobe and slippers. She was pretty, even without makeup, about five-five, very thin, with light brown hair. She stepped outside and closed the door behind her.

She smiled at me.

I smiled back at her, grabbed both her skinny wrists with one hand and kicked the door in. The Ugly American.

Door splinters flew everywhere. Charlotte screamed

as I passed her off to Sylvia, who came alive and clamped the thrashing mom in a headlock.

I spotted a phone on a small table in the foyer and ripped it from the wall. The screams must have alerted Jerry and Hondo because they both came charging into the house. The grandmother was standing in front of a crib. When she saw Jerry and realized what was happening, she reached into the crib and picked up the little boy. Jerry lunged for his son. He and Granny were engaged in a tug-of-war with the little guy. I knew that if this kept up, *both* families would have the child, only he'd be in two pieces.

That's when Jerry slugged Granny. A roundhouse to the jaw. Down went Granny, releasing the boy. Jerry held him up like a football. The kid was wailing. Hondo whizzed by me toward a stairway.

At the top of the stairs stood the grandfather. In one hand was a cordless phone. The other held a shotgun. Hondo was inching up the stairs toward the old man.

"C'mon, Pop, gimme the gun before I shove it up your ass."

Good going, Hondo, piss the guy off. Grandpop wasn't all that old, I figured about sixty and in pretty good shape. His eyes were bulging. He dropped the phone and leveled the shotgun at Hondo.

"Put the boy down!" he screamed. "I called the police, they're on their way!"

The boy was thrashing in Jerry's arms, Charlotte and Sylvia were rolling around on the floor, and Hondo was looking down the barrel of a double-barreled shotgun. Granny was groaning and starting to get up. I inched up the stairs and stood next to Hondo. I raised both hands.

"Easy, sir," I said calmly. "We're from the American

embassy. If you fire that gun, you'll create an international incident." I lifted my jacket. "I'm not armed."

The grandfather swallowed hard. "You're full of shit!" he said in flawless English. "Put down my grandson!" Hondo and I went up a step. We were no more than five feet from the end of the barrel.

"DON'T MOVE!" the guy bellowed.

I heard movement behind us. Granny was on her feet and grappling with Jerry. Sylvia was still going two out of three falls with Charlotte. Jerry shoved Granny to the floor and bolted for the door with the kid.

The radio in my pocket blared. "Everything okay down there?" It was Beau, obviously worried. I heard sirens in the distance. Everything's just ducky, I thought.

The old man heard the sirens, too, and was momentarily distracted as he glanced toward a hallway window.

Hondo jumped him. The shotgun discharged into the ceiling, sending bits of plaster cascading down like giant snowflakes. Hondo landed a short right to the grandfather's jaw. The old man hit the carpeting like a bundle of rags. He'd be a little sore tomorrow but otherwise all right. I crushed the portable phone under a size eleven.

"Let's get the hell out of here!" I yelled. Hondo and I tumbled down the last few stairs and rolled right into Sylvia and Charlotte, who were still tussling. I picked Charlotte up and tossed her on a couch. She was exhausted and didn't follow us.

Jerry was already in the backseat of the car with his son. The boy had calmed down and was smiling. I took the wheel, with Hondo next to me and Sylvia in the back. I left a cloud of dust and was on my way before the doors had shut.

Beau was screaming on the radio, "What the fuck happened down there!?" He must have seen the police cars speeding to the scene.

We were all knocked out. I didn't feel like explaining. "We're okay, we got the kid. Bring the chopper down, we'll be there in three minutes." I was doing at least ninety.

"Well, you better speed it up," Beau said, "because you've got a caravan of radio cars heading right for you." He was trying to sound calm, but there was an edge to his voice. "Listen to me, Wags, you gotta get to the turnoff in the landing area before the cops pass it. If they do, you're fucked."

Now I was scared. I was on a straightaway and I could see the flashing lights of the police vehicles in the distance. I floored the rented car and cursed the fact that we hadn't sprung for a car with a bigger engine. The car inched ahead faster, to about 100 miles per hour.

Sylvia was screaming for me to slow down. Hondo was telling me to speed up. Jerry was saying "Oh, God!" over and over. I heard nothing from the boy. Sweat poured into my eyes. It burned like hell but I didn't dare take a hand off the wheel to wipe it away.

We were about a quarter mile from the closest police car when I overshot the turnoff to the field where Beau waited in a grounded, idling helicopter.

"Sonofabitch!" I screamed. I jammed on the brakes and backed up in a cloud of dust. I couldn't see shit but I executed a bootleg turn like I'd been taught in the police academy and swung around onto the access road. Who says you forget everything you learn in the academy?

My momentary elation was short-lived. A string of radio cars turned in right after me, most veering out of control. The few seconds it took to steer into their skids gave us precious time to gain distance.

The helicopter was hovering about a foot off the ground when we slid up to it. My passengers were out of the car before it stopped. Beau jumped from the chopper and boosted Sylvia inside. Then it was Hondo's turn, then Jerry with the baby, then me.

The first cop car roared into the clearing. Two cops flew out with guns drawn. I was in the helicopter and grabbed Beau by the wrist. "Time to go home."

The chopper lifted off. Beau was dangling. I held on tight and pulled. Beau went flying into the bird, landing on an exhausted Sylvia. We were in the air.

We lay there motionless for what seemed like minutes. I saw at least six more radio cars circle our abandoned car like marauding Apaches. The pilot banked a hard left. We were on our way to Germany.

There were a few anxious minutes at the Hamburg airport, but we boarded a jet with no problems. Apparently the Danish cops were looking for us in Denmark. We finally settled down after we'd cleared European airspace. Then the giddiness began.

A risky operation does that to a person. Even in the police department, after a particularly adrenaline-pumping arrest, cops find it difficult to wind down or spend time with people other than cops. You've got to share the excitement with someone who was there. Even Sylvia was high-fiving everybody. We were blabbing like we were high on drugs. But as fast as we'd gone up, we crashed down. We were all unconscious one hour into the flight. I slept like a dead man.

My stomach tightened a bit at customs after we landed at JFK, but we passed through with no problems. All I wanted to do was get home to my family. Beau had a limo waiting for us. He always did treat his people well.

Before we were able to get in the car, Jerry got teary-eyed and embraced each of us individually. I felt good about what I'd done and I'm sure the feeling was the same for the rest of the crew.

You know, it's funny, I was turning into a real money-aware guy, but on this job I wasn't concerned with a profit. After expenses, we each got a thousand dollars. Maybe that would cover my dry-cleaning bill. Beau, I heard, gave his profit back to Jerry. I went home feeling good about myself.

Jerry still has his son. I hear the kid's doing fine and I hear from Jerry every so often. He has no contact with his wife but it wouldn't surprise me if she makes a grab for the boy sometime in the future. We'll be there for him. Nothing came of our little adventure, no charges filed, no international indignation. Just a little dispute between ex-lovers.

chapter three

I spent a few quiet weeks at home. Things had finally slowed down a little but I still had checks coming in from old jobs. Enrolling my kids in private schools had become a reality. I was also able to take my wife out to nice places, something she deserved after raising four kids (and me). On the downside, I now had an improved lifestyle that I enjoyed but that required me to pull in large fees to keep me from sliding back into post-police-department penny-pinching.

Now I was definitely the person to call if you wanted someone snatched. Unfortunately, most of the calls came from sources not generally associated with legality. I was turning down work from mob-connected people who wanted people taken off the street so they could have a "private talk" with them. I wasn't so mercenary at that time that I was close to tempted to become a full-time law breaker. That would come later.

There were plenty of people in my business who would accept a legitimate child-custody job but I was viewed as someone who would do more than talk a good case. I would take the extra chance to make certain it all came together successfully. It all came back to my thirst for thrills and my desire to right what I considered a wrong no matter what the risk. I guess that's a fancy way to say I can be pigheaded at times when I feel I have to do the right thing.

I remember one particular incident when I was working in the Ninth Precinct, in the East Village. Also known as "Alphabet City" because the streets are designated by letters, the neighborhood was one of the toughest in the city, if not the country. Any cop who showed any sign of weakness was in for trouble. There was a gang member there we called Little Man, a misnomer if there ever was one. Little Man was my height and outweighed me by thirty pounds. He was a mean street punk who dealt drugs and mugged people. The word on the street was that he was responsible for more than his share of killings. Little Man took it upon himself to taunt every cop in the precinct. He would curse cops in public because he knew we couldn't do anything about it in front of witnesses. He tossed bricks off roofs in an effort to kill us. Not a nice person.

Finally, I had had enough. One night on a late tour— midnight to eight for you civilians—I slipped out of my uniform while I was on duty and waited in a doorway on a street inhabited by predators. I knew Little Man would pass by sooner or later. I froze in that doorway for over six hours until the miscreant walked by me and I pounced on him. I beat the miserable bastard to within an inch of his life using just my fists because it was the right thing to do. Cops have to survive on the street. The Job is not a rerun of *Barney Miller*. It's a shame that violence is all that someone like Little Man understands, but after our encounter he respected me and the cops I worked with. He steered clear of us. Score one for the good guys.

About a month after Denmark, I had had just about all the downtime I could handle. Finally, something came along that wouldn't get me ten years in Attica. A wealthy investment banker called me and asked if I could forcibly remove his girlfriend from her estate in Connecticut and deliver her to a mental institution in Manhattan. The girlfriend, he explained, was a German actress of some repute who was in her late fifties and was experiencing psychological problems. She had locked herself in her house and refused to come out. For anybody, boyfriend included. All her food was delivered. She had no friends in this country other than my new client and he was concerned that she might be a hazard to herself.

I met with the client in his office in Midtown. He was in his early sixties and dressed for the part of a wealthy banker: navy blue three-piece suit, rep tie, and dark brown oxfords. I wanted to tell him about the existence of navy blue shoes but he probably wouldn't want to break up the look. I mentally calculated tuition, car and mortgage payments, dinner at the Four Seasons for me and my wife weekly for the foreseeable future, divided by two, and came up with a decent figure for a retainer. Apparently I could have thrown in the down payment on a small boat because my client whipped out a roll of cash and peeled off a pile of hundreds like he was dealing cards. Somehow I thought that I was seeing the skim from his clients' investments. Anyway, I was in business.

On any assignment where force may be necessary

and particularly where a mentally disturbed person is involved, it's wise to enlist help. This help should come from an individual possessing good verbal skills and a friendly yet persuasive nature.

So I called Hondo.

I offered him eight hundred dollars for the day.

"Who we gotta kill?" he asked. A true humanitarian. I filled him in on the details and while he bitched that an Armani suit costs two grand I countered by telling him the job would only last a matter of hours and we were dealing with an older woman, not Hannibal Lecter. Even Hondo can be reasonable.

The following day we drove to the woman's fashionable Connecticut address and scouted the area. Her home was set off the road but within eyeball distance of neighbors on either side. It was midsummer but there were no kids playing outside and only a few cars parked in adjacent driveways.

Hondo was dressed in his Armani uniform of the day. That morning I had chosen a conservative dark brown Brooks Brothers suit, white shirt, and boring paisley tie. I figured, Why upset the woman with flash? The plan was simple. Aren't they all?

Before we left New York I had my client give me a check made out to his nutty girlfriend for ten grand. Her birthday was in two weeks but I figured an early ten-thousand-dollar gift wouldn't be turned away. Once she accepted the check, I'd make a grab for her. We took handcuffs and three bedsheets with us. We'd cuff the old bat, then wrap her up like a salami. What could be simpler?

She answered the door wearing a ratty housecoat over a nightgown. She was barefoot.

"Yes?" she said warily through a screen door. She

was tall, about five-eight, with a scarecrow's face and long scraggly gray hair that looked like she'd just ridden in on the wing of a 747. She looked ten years older than her age and spoke with a slight German accent. I have no idea what my client saw in her unless he had a *Whatever Happened to Baby Jane?* fetish. All the woman needed was an ax and a target.

I introduced myself and told her that her boyfriend had asked me to deliver an envelope to her. I held it up.

She eyed me like a suspicious animal. "You will open it, please?" With a German accent it sounded like a command from a storm trooper.

I did as I was told and waved the check in front of her nose. She opened the door cautiously and made a grab for the check. I grabbed a bony wrist. She kicked me in the balls. I let go of her wrist. The chase was on.

The woman could run. She flew through the house like a gazelle, but aching gonads or not, I was right behind her. Hondo was right behind me, cursing. I heard him slip and fall on a scatter rug but he was up in a flash.

There was a screen door in the back of the house. The woman pushed it open and raced through the yard, screaming at the top of her lungs. You've gotta picture this nut galloping across her yard, robe billowing in the wind, rat's-nest hair caught in the updraft and this high-pitched screech. She looked like she should be chasing *us*. I caught the door as it was swinging shut and pounded it open. The door was spring-loaded and came back square in Hondo's face. He went right through the screen like it was fog. Never even slowed him down.

By this time the galloping granny was beyond her

yard and rampaging through the woods, still hollering. The previous day I had done heavy leg squats in the gym and my thighs were on fire. Every stride I took was hurting more and the old lady was putting more distance between us. I was praying that her neighbors weren't home to see two grown men chasing this wacko through the brush.

I heard a grunt behind me and caught a glimpse of Hondo as he passed me. I could tell he was pissed. He emitted some kind of ear-shattering war cry—something the Rangers must have taught him to do when he was shooting Ethiopians—and pounced on the old lady as she was about to scale a fence.

The woman fought like we were dragging her to the electric chair. She kicked, spat and took a chunk out of Hondo's shoulder with some very real teeth. We'd left the sheets in the car, not anticipating the steeplechase, and had to make do with cuffing her. Hondo tossed her over his shoulder—the one that wasn't bleeding—and we made it back to the car. I have to admit, I was winded. My legs ached. Hondo's face looked like a tennis racket. I had had an easier time going head-to-head with Little Man.

While Hondo sat on her in the backseat of the car, I went back into the house with the sheets and soaked them in the tub. I secured the house before we left. It took the two of us five minutes to wrap the sheets around Battling Bertha. Hondo stayed in the backseat with her when we finally headed back to New York.

My heart finally stopped racing on the Merritt Parkway. The woman still had energy but would tire quickly during attempts to escape. We learned a lot of German curses that day. I thought we were home free when a tractor-trailer pulled up alongside us and the driver glanced in my car.

Our trussed package in the backseat spotted the driver looking at us and started fighting like mad. She managed to throw her legs over the seat back and kick me in the head. I temporarily lost control of the car and swerved dangerously close to the truck. The driver blared his air horn. I had to give Hondo credit for restraint. He was trying to use his body weight to subdue the woman but I saw it wasn't working. Any minute I expected him to cold-cock her and we'd be delivering a comatose German to our client.

I was momentarily distracted by the truck driver.

He had his CB radio microphone in his hand. The driver was calling the cops!

I immediately saw myself being led off to jail. Over twenty years on The Job, and I had never come close to being locked up. I had just survived a close encounter with the Danish police and now some German horror actress was going to be the cause of my downfall.

Instinctively, I went for my duplicate shield. Every retired cop has a dupe shield made before he gets out. It comes in handy when stopped for speeding, when identifying yourself to police officers, and it provides a basic security blanket and link to The Job. I don't believe it's ever been used to get out of a kidnapping charge.

I lowered my window and waved the tin at the trucker. I yelled, "NYPD. She's a prisoner!" These days such a scene would almost ensure a special prosecutor and an indictment for torturing a prisoner but a few years ago the NYPD still enjoyed a quasi-respectable reputation. The Job was between scandals.

It worked. The trucker hesitated a minute, then

smiled and waved. My heart went back to its normal pace. We were going to make it. From the backseat an exhausted Hondo said, "Can we kill her now?"

"You do it," I said, "I'm too tired."

When we approached toll booths, Hondo slid our charge to the floor and sat on her. Thank God I'd brought exact change. We made one stop at a phone to alert our client that we were on our way. I drove my car down a ramp at a private hospital off Fifth Avenue. Our client was waiting at the bottom with three gorillas in white hospital garb. Our package had lost her spirit and was docile as we unloaded her onto a gurney. Mr. Cool Banker broke down when he saw her condition. He wiped his tears away with a silk handkerchief.

"She was really beautiful once," he said.

Yeah, I thought, so was Bette Davis. He paid us cash on the spot. I gave Hondo an extra two hundred. He grunted. "Do me a favor," he said through clenched teeth, "the next time you want to call me—don't." I couldn't blame him.

I vowed then and there that I'd done my last kidnapping. I couldn't imagine any circumstances that would make me change my mind.

Istanbul changed all that.

chapter four

I was asleep when the phone rang. The bedroom was inky dark. My wife was sleeping soundly. Cops' wives learn to sleep through late-night phone calls. For a split second, I thought I was still on The Job.

"Hello," I rasped. Gotta get off the Luckys.

"Wags? Fred Cavalcante."

My eyes finally focused on my watch. Three in the morning. Freddy was a detective in a Brooklyn South precinct detective squad. We had worked together briefly and had remained friends. "Uh," I said. My bubbly personality doesn't kick into gear until I've had my coffee.

"Listen, I hate to call you so late—or so early—whatever, but I think I got something you might be interested in." His tone was conspiratorial. I figured he was at work. I sat bolt upright and shook my head. Cobwebs flew. I told him to hold on while I took the call in the kitchen.

I cradled the phone next to my ear and wandered

around the kitchen collecting coffee fixings. I had lived in the house for nineteen years and the kitchen was still uncharted territory—unless I was making sauce. Tomato paste and garlic I could find.

The coffee perked. I had something to live for. "Whaddaya have?" For a working detective to call me at that hour, I was sure it had to be important.

"Listen, I'm signing out early—using some lost time—meet me where we used to go."

We used to go a lot of places but I assumed that at this hour he wasn't referring to the topless bar on Nostrand Avenue. We were silent for a while, one cop's paranoia traveling by osmosis to another. "Got it."

The diner off the Belt Parkway was crowded at four A.M. It was a Tuesday morning but Brooklyn wiseguys liked to say they only partied on days ending in *y*. The bars had just closed and the people who weren't high on coke were shoveling down scrambled eggs. Booths were jammed with mobster wanna-bes all dressed alike in jeans, white T-shirts, and sport jackets. Each sported a ninety-mile-an-hour haircut and Mr. T starter-set gold chains. The women all looked like Fran Drescher on a bad-hair day. Cigarette smoke hung heavy and there was a steady stream of bodies going back and forth to the bathroom to vacuum up the last of the night's stash. I spotted Freddy hunkered over a coffee cup. I motioned to the parking lot.

We sat in my car. Freddy handed me a cardboard container. I peeled back a portion of the plastic lid and slurped weak coffee. "I think I'm in a time warp," I said, suddenly remembering that it wasn't so long ago that I'd sat on stakeouts inhaling coffee to stay awake. "What's up?"

"I caught a real bad one. Guy beat the shit out of his

wife with a hammer." Freddy was dressed in a leather blazer, gray slacks, and a blue silk shirt. I hadn't seen him in about a year and he looked as sharp as ever.

"I hate to be callous, but it's after four in the morning. Thanks for sharing, but so what?"

"There's a kid involved."

Freddy had nine kids. I remembered that once we'd broken into his locker and stapled closed all the zippers on his pants. Police humor. Kids were Freddy's life. He's the only cop I know who would rather watch the Smurfs with his children on Saturday morning than play golf. I always had great admiration for him. I figured I was about to hear a horror story. "Tell me about it."

Freddy related a real soap opera. An Italian woman from Borough Park, Rosemary, had married a Turkish citizen, Hasan. The marriage was one of convenience, at least for Hasan. He married the rather rotund and unattractive Rosemary to freeload off her. He was illegal and had no intention of working. Almost from the beginning, Hasan beat the hell out of Rosemary. He hit her with anything he could get his hands on—wooden planks, pipes, hammers, etc. A son was eventually born. I guess Hasan didn't know he was only supposed to knock Rosemary *down*. The day little Hossi entered the world, Daddy took off.

"It was good riddance, as far as the mother was concerned," Freddy said. "Then, the day the kid turned seven, Hasan reappeared. He came back to New York through Canada."

"Is seven years old significant?" I asked.

"Yeah, according to Islamic law, the day a boy turns seven he becomes a man."

So now, Freddy says, Hasan makes nice-nice and

gets back with the hapless Rosemary, who thinks everything is going to be okay. Hasan stays with her about six months and things seem to be going well. No more beatings, just a little verbal abuse. Hasan had a master plan, it seemed, and he didn't want to create any problems until it was implemented. At about this time he suggests to Rosemary that little Hossi visit his family in Turkey. Hasan says that his mother is very sick and wants to see her grandson. Rosemary agrees. They get the kid a passport and hire a Turkish nanny to escort the kid on the plane to Istanbul. The trip is supposed to last a week.

"They get to JFK, the kid gets on the plane." Freddy downed the last of the coffee. "The kid's in the air, Hasan turns to Rosemary and says, 'Fuck you, you're never seeing Hossi again.' Rosemary starts to balk, Hasan lays her out right in the terminal. Then he tells her Hossi will grow up to be a great soldier and hate all Americans."

"Nice guy."

"For the next two weeks, the mother pleads with Hasan to have the kid returned. Every time she mouths off, Hasan decks her, usually with whatever's handy. She doesn't know what to do so she goes to the cops. I catch the case."

"Did you lock up Hasan?"

"For what?" Freddy said. "The DA won't touch the Turkey thing, some shit about creating an international incident. We got a warrant out for him on the assault. He's in the wind."

"Try the American embassy?"

"They faded. All talk at the beginning but nothing at the wire. Some suit said that since the kid's father is a Turkish citizen, once the kid's in Turkey we can't touch him. Technically it's not kidnapping, it's custodial interference when a parent is involved. As it stands now, the kid's stuck there."

"What can I do about it?" I knew what was coming.

Freddy looked at me. "I heard about Denmark."

There's no one sharper than a New York City detective. I'm convinced that if a bunch of retired detectives from The Job had worked for Nixon during the Watergate scandal, we'd be seeing him on taped footage kissing Ronald Reagan on both cheeks when he left office after two successful terms, while Jimmy Carter shucked peanuts.

I shook my head. "Oh, no. I'm done with that stuff." Connecticut was still fresh in my mind. "I'm trying to make it as a PI." We argued for an hour. Finally he convinced me to meet Rosemary before I made my final decision.

Rosemary was staying with her parents in Canarsie. She was a mass of scrapes and black-and-blue marks. Her face was puffy from constant beatings. She looked more like Jake LaMotta than a thirty-year-old mother. Then there were the tears. I hate the tears. Apparently, Freddy had told her I was her savior. Within five minutes she was clutching my arm and wailing, "My baby, my baby!" Ten minutes after that I was reassuring her that I would get little Hossi back. Goddamn Freddy.

She had scraped together ten thousand dollars. I hated taking it, but I had to put together a team and get us over there. Freddy, as he put it, didn't want a "hat," cop talk for a kickback, for getting me the job.

The first thing I needed was volunteers. I made phone calls for three days and got nowhere. Everybody I spoke to reminded me of the movie *Midnight Express.* I still had my ace in the hole. I made the call.

"Yo, Hondo, wanna go to Istanbul and kidnap a kid?"

"We gonna be back by next Friday? I got a tailor's appointment."

"I'll work on it."

"Yeah, sure." Not a moment's hesitation. There was no mention of the Connecticut fiasco.

Rosemary had memorized a phone number belongings to Hasan's uncle that Hasan called in Istanbul. I utilized a reverse phone directory computer database and came up with an address. At least we had a place to start. Next we had to neutralize Hasan.

When Rosemary went to the police, Hasan vanished, figuring he would be locked up for assault at least. My feeling was that he knew he was home free on the custodial-interference charge. But there was a warrant for his arrest on second-degree assault. The police rarely look for anyone wanted on an outstanding warrant unless it's a publicized case. Usually, fugitives get picked up on an unrelated charge and when their name is run through the NCIC computer in Washington, D.C., the outstanding warrant will surface. No one was actively looking for Hasan, and I was afraid that he might get wind of our operation and alert his family in Turkey if he was permitted to remain free.

Freddy made copies of the picture of Hasan he'd gotten from Rosemary and distributed them to every cop in Brooklyn South. He did this on his own time. That section of Brooklyn is predominantly Italian and Hasan stuck out like a falafel in a sea of meatballs. He was picked up in two days. We got to a friendly judge to set a high bail. We figured we had two weeks before Hasan's court-appointed lawyer got the bail reduced or had him released on his own recognizance. We knew that if he got to Turkey, we'd never get the kid back.

Hondo and I left for Istanbul via London. We had about eight thousand dollars in cash with us for expenses, but this job wasn't about money. I could still hear Hossi's mother crying and calling his name. The father was a mutt and Istanbul was no place to raise a kid. My heart ached for the little boy. Eventually, the job would cost us money.

Istanbul is really two cities, the new and the old. I would categorize the new city as New York's Lower East Side after a typhoon. And this is the part the Turks are proud of. The old city is literally thousands of years old and separated from the new city by a rusted bridge. The old city reminded me of the South Bronx with no paved roads. Genuine urban squalor coupled with foul air. The place smelled like a sewer. At least in the Bronx you smelled all that good Puerto Rican food. Here, no matter where you went, all you smelled was human waste. There was mud everywhere. The streets were so narrow that sunlight hit the ground for only a few minutes a day so the mud remained just that, muddy. And it was hot, was it ever hot. I had been there briefly many years before while I was in the navy and had forgotten the intense humidity. Hondo had enough sense to board his Armani wardrobe and traveled light. "I was in Ethiopia, man, I know heat," he said. We stayed in the Hilton Hotel in the new city.

Our first stop after checking into our hotel was the American embassy. An assistant to an assistant ambassador, Roger Daley, ushered us into his office. We identified ourselves as security consultants. He checked our IDs.

"And what can I do for you gentlemen?" he said. His office was pleasantly air-conditioned and located in a compound in the center of the new city. Machine gun–toting marines guarded the perimeter. *Semper fi*. He was a career foreign-service officer about forty years old dressed in khaki slacks and a striped short-sleeved blue shirt. No tie. It must have been casual Friday.

I was straight with him. I explained the background of the case and that we were in Istanbul to return the child to his mother.

Daley smiled. "And how do you propose to go about it?"

Hondo cut in. "We figured we snatch the fucking kid and fly the hell out of this cesspool." Not much chance of Hondo becoming a diplomat.

Daley was appalled. "Are you men out of your mind? This isn't the States. You get caught doing that here and you'll be in jail for three years before you ever get to arraignment." He made the now familiar reference to *Midnight Express*. "I can help you within these walls, but you do what you're thinking of doing and you're on your own. By the way, I trust that neither of you is armed?"

Hondo gave him a look as if to say, "Hey man, I *am* a lethal weapon."

"No weapons," I said, sorry I hadn't at least brought a good knife.

"Good. Get caught with a gun here and you'll never get home."

Daley was as helpful as he could be without sanctioning what we were going to do. He gave us a map and showed us, based on the address we supplied, where Hasan's uncle lived. He even called a cab for us and told the driver in Turkish to take us to the address. The cab was able to get about a quarter mile from the house. The mud made getting any closer impossible. We were literally ankle deep in slop. Hondo ruined a pair of Ferragamos; he was pissed. The house was more of a dried mud shack jammed in the middle of hundreds of houses that looked just like it. The smell was overwhelming. There was no way we could grab the kid and make a fast getaway without getting bogged down. We would need a Humvee and a platoon of Rangers to run interference. We went back to the hotel and had a strategy meeting.

It was decided that attempting to grab the boy without help would be next to impossible. We called the desk and inquired about the services of an interpreter. They had no one on staff, but the desk clerk said his cousin could speak excellent English and was discreet. I asked that he come up.

The interpreter could most kindly be described as a bag of shit. His name was Gunyon and he was about thirty years old and dressed in filthy American-style clothes. His pants were ripped and so soiled I wasn't sure of their color. His shirt was so dirty it could have stood in a corner by itself. His body odor could have cleared out a room of skunks. His skin and beard looked as if they hadn't been washed in weeks. All this and he wanted a hundred dollars a day. My feeling was that he'd never seen that kind of money but he knew we were up to no good and that was his price. We hired him on the spot.

We sat Gunyon as far from us as we could and devised a plan. We'd go to the cops and try to bribe *them* to grab the kid. From what I remembered about Turkey, every cop was corrupt. We bounced the idea off the smelly one.

"Not so good."

Hondo and I exchanged glances. "Why the hell not?" I asked.

"In this country, Mr. Wags, the judicial system works in the opposite way it does in America. Correct me if I'm wrong, but don't you go to the police with a complaint in your country and *then* they take it to the prosecutor?"

"Right."

"Here," Gunyon said, "you go to the prosecutor *first*. They determine if you have a case, *then* you go to the police."

Hondo said, "We're looking to bribe some cops, not solve a crime."

Gunyon grinned, not a pretty sight. "First you must bribe the prosecutor."

We spent two days with the local prosecutor, who, coincidentally, was Gunyon's cousin. We filled out a mountain of paperwork, greased the DA, or whatever you call him over there, five hundred dollars, and took the forms to the police station that covers the area where Hossi's uncle lived.

The police station made the inside of a garbage can look like a hospital operating room. I was afraid to sit down or lean against anything. The cop who took the paperwork was a cousin of Gunyon's. What a surprise. He spoke no English. Gunyon said his cousin would go to the uncle's house and demand the boy.

We went outside and the cop hailed a beat-up old cab. It seemed they didn't have radio cars. We cabbed it as close as we could get to the uncle's house and stood behind the cop while he spoke to the uncle in Turkish. I don't know how the cop explained our presence but the uncle didn't seem concerned about us. While the two of them were rattling on, I whispered to Gunyon to get us in the house. He stood mum and let his cousin the cop do the talking. Later we found out that the uncle had Hossi hidden in a drawer in the house while he was telling the cop that the kid wasn't there.

We wound up back at the police station. Gunyon explained to us that his cousin wouldn't go into the uncle's house without permission from his superior. My bullshit radar kicked in. The shakedown was about to rear its ugly head.

A lieutenant appeared who spoke passable English. He told us that, if at all possible, he would like to go back and get the boy that day. This was going to cost us a thousand dollars, American.

I balked. "We've alerted the uncle. The kid, if he was there, is probably in the mountains hidden under a pile of goat shit by now."

The lieutenant smiled. At least he had teeth, probably purchased with American bribes. "No matter. I'm certain the uncle will cooperate and tell us where he is."

I gave the lieutenant ten hundred-dollar bills and the five of us got another cab and went back to the house. The uncle was about fifty, fat and wearing the official Turkish cologne, Essence of Body Odor. As soon as he opened the door he knew he was in for trouble.

The lieutenant didn't ask him anything. He took out a blackjack and smashed the poor bastard across the nose. The uncle went down amid tears and blood. We dragged him into the hovel. While the cops held him down, Hondo and I searched the house. The floors were dirt, and the furniture, what there was of it, was moldy and crumbling. The place consisted of one big room divided by curtains to form a sort of Turkish version of a studio apartment.

We tossed the place good but didn't come up with the kid. There was filth and vermin everywhere. The toilet consisted of a hole in the ground. There were rags hanging over an iron bar to clean with and a rubber hose with a trickle of putrid water spilling out with which to wash. I wished I had brought rubber gloves. I had the urge to take a very hot shower. I thought of an American child living under those conditions and now *I* felt like smacking the uncle around.

I emerged through a curtain. The lieutenant looked up.

"No kid," I said.

The beating continued for at least another thirty minutes. I could tell the cops had done this before. They hit the uncle hard enough to cause pain and draw blood but not enough to render him unconscious or kill him. This takes talent.

The uncle swore through cracked lips that he didn't know where the boy was. He admitted that he had been there but that a cousin had taken the kid after we'd left the first time. No amount of punishment could budge him. Maybe he was telling the truth.

We went back every day for the next four days. Every day it cost us another grand. Usually the uncle was there by himself and he would catch another beating. One day a neighbor was with him, probably someone the uncle disliked, who he'd invited over for some Turkish coffee and a beating. The neighbor got banged around for being in the wrong place at the wrong time. He didn't know anything either.

By this time we were running out of money. We're paying Ali Baba and the Forty Thieves one large a day and nothing's getting done. The uncle was resigned to getting his daily beating and took it like a man. We decided to take a different approach.

I figured there had to be a Turkish version of the Mafia, the problem being how to find it. The cops administered beatings; maybe some connected Turks could apply another kind of pressure on the uncle. For three days we prowled the back streets of the old city looking for the Turkish John Gotti. During this time, by the way, Hondo sampled every kind of Turkish cuisine he could find from street vendors. Some of the crap he ate looked like it had passed the spoiled stage during the last war. He had to brush flies from most of the food. I ate only in the hotel. I wound up with constant stomach trouble and Hondo never even burped. He couldn't wait to get out every day and sample some rancid meat. God bless him.

We were finally directed to a bar, if you could call it that, in what had to be the most down-trodden area on earth. In it we were told we could find Callah, a genuine gangster, Turkish style. The bar was about the size of a Fotomat, made of wood, rags, and with a nice coating of mud and human feces. We were told that the latter made excellent cement. I'd remember that the next time I changed my grandson's diaper.

Callah turned out to be something out of central casting. He was somewhere between thirty and sixty—it was difficult to tell his age because of the grime and dirt that filled in the cracks in his face. It had to be over a hundred degrees in that rat hole but

Callah wore a long-flowing, crud-covered *wool* robe and scuffed boots. He smoked a joint as thick as a cigar. Perched on his head was a Bonomo's Turkish taffy hat complete with the little tassel thing hanging from it. I expected Sydney Greenstreet to come walking in at any moment with a Maltese falcon under one arm.

Callah was a bullshitter extraordinaire who spoke passable English. He promised us the kid delivered to our hotel the next day. Of course, this was going to cost us two thousand dollars. Before we blew the guy off I wanted to pick his brain for any information or ideas we could get for free. We spent two hours with him and drank some kind of local drink that had me hallucinating after the first twenty minutes. Sooner or later I knew I would have to use the bathroom and I wasn't looking forward to it. Finally, I could wait no longer and staggered into the can.

The floor was the usual mud accompanied by what looked like the same dirty rags that had been in the uncle's house. Maybe they shared them. So there I was peeing in this little hole in the ground when I glanced over at the rotten wooden wall next to me. I saw initials and a date carved into the wood: JJW '66. My initials! I had been in that cesspool while I was in the navy, probably looking to get laid. I assume I didn't or my genitals would probably have fallen off. Just goes to show you what three months at sea will do to a twenty-year-old sailor. I went back to Hondo and Callah. They were still sucking down the Turkish potion. Hondo was eating some mystery meat that still seemed alive.

"Let's go. This is getting too weird." I grabbed Hondo by the shirt and dragged him out of there.

We went back to the hotel and counted our money. We had less than two thousand left. We knew that once the cash went, so would the police cooperation. I got hold of Gunyon and offered a deal.

"Listen, suppose we stake out the uncle's house with your cousin the cop. He's gotta be seeing the kid or going to some member of the family who perhaps can't take the punishment he can. What's it gonna cost us to sit on the uncle? Flat rate."

Gunyon made a phone call. "Five thousand, American."

Hondo added his two cents. "What are you, fucking crazy?"

"Mr. Hondo, the lieutenant has to be included."

We told Gunyon to wait in the hall. We'd already invested eight thousand dollars and had gotten nowhere. We knew if we staked out the uncle long enough, he would lead us to the kid. The only problem was, we didn't have five grand. I would have to call the client. I called her at her parents' house and explained the problem. She said she would have the money to us in about a day.

"Tell your cousin it's a deal," I told Gunyon. "We have to wait a day." Maybe he would buy some soap with his end.

The next day came and went. No money. I called Rosemary. No answer at her parents' house. Around noon the following day there was a knock on our door. I opened it to face a sweating Rosemary.

"Hi!" she said.

"Hi? What the hell are you doing here?" I looked in the hall behind her. "There anyone with you?"

"No, just me. I couldn't bear being away from my little boy." She looked like a dejected basset hound.

"Christ!" I hollered. She winced.

Hondo came strolling out of the bathroom in his underwear. "You got the money?" Right to the point.

Rosemary lifted her skirt. It was hard to determine which I wanted to see less, Gunyon's teeth or what I was currently looking at. But her panty hose were stuffed with bills. "Five thousand," she said. She started removing the bills. Hondo went back to the bathroom.

After she dumped the money on my bed, I asked, "What room are you in?"

"Room?" The hotel, she said, was full. She was going to stay with us.

I was damned if I was going to give up my bed. I knew Hondo would want to keep his bed, which was closer to the window. He would get up in the middle of the night to pee out of it. He'd mutter, "Fucking rag heads," and get back in bed. I think he was sleep-pissing.

We partitioned off part of the room with sheets and got a cot from Gunyon's cousin. Not the cop, the desk clerk. Rosemary was content with the setup but I wanted to get the job done and get the hell out of there as soon as possible.

We paid the cops off the next morning. The lieutenant and Gunyon's cousin the cop didn't acknowledge Rosemary's presence. Women are considered non-people in Turkey. I think Rosemary was used to it. We sat on the uncle's hovel for two days in a taxi (more money). Finally, on the third day, the uncle left in a cab. We followed him for two hours to a remote village in the mountains. He entered a clone of all the other houses we'd seen and didn't come out. The village was tiny, maybe forty homes, if you could call them that, with a lot of women scurrying about. We saw no men. They were probably attending pickpockets' school.

After three hours, Hondo had had enough. "Fuck it, let's go in." He started to get out of the cab.

I grabbed his arm. "Hold up. The kid may not be in there."

"So what're we gonna do, sit here another three hours?" He had a point. It was real raw in that car.

I sighed. "Okay, let's do it." Rosemary stayed in the cab with the driver while Hondo, the two cops, Gunyon, and myself broke right through the door of the house.

The uncle and another man, who turned out to be yet another cousin, were sitting at a table in the middle of the room. Sheets hung around the room separating the living quarters from the eating area. It looked like the same decorator had been retained by the entire family. The uncle and the other man were startled. The uncle spotted the cops and muttered what must have been the equivalent of "Oh shit!" in Turkish. He ran for the rear of the house. Hondo grabbed him before he made it.

The cousin started screaming even before anyone touched him. Our weak link. Gunyon's cousin smacked him across the face and rattled something off in Turkish. The man pointed outside. The lieutenant waved a hand, saying, "Mr. Wags, follow me."

We found Hossi in the house next door, playing with two little girls. He was filthy but seemed happy. I scooped him up under an arm and got him outside. Rosemary saw her son and ran to him from the cab. The mother and son reunion made all the bullshit we had had to endure that week worth the effort. Hossi was so happy to see his mom that we couldn't pry them apart. After nearly squashing her son, she embraced *me* and wouldn't let go. Villagers were starting to congregate. "We should get out of here." I looked around to gather the crew. Hondo was missing.

I found him in the shack holding a switchblade on the uncle and the cousin, both of whom were nursing head wounds. "Where'd you get the knife?"

"Don't ask."

The cops read the two men the riot act. They were harangued in Turkish but I got the drift. Make a stink about what just happened and die. The universal language.

Hossi stayed with us in our room at the Hilton that night. He had been in Turkey a very short time but already he had some remarks about Americans that weren't very flattering. His uncle had begun the brainwashing process as soon as Hossi's little feet hit the mud in his new home. I was sure that he would get back to being a normal American kid when he got home.

The homecoming was a circus. I had called Freddy before we departed Istanbul and he had contacted the American embassy to apprise them of our success. Apparently someone in the embassy thought it would be a good idea to alert the press. Naturally, a photo op like this couldn't be passed up by politicians.

When we got off the plane at JFK, we were met by a goddamn oompah band and an army of journalists. There was a United States senator in attendance, who undoubtedly wanted to take the credit for getting Hossi out of Turkey. He had done it before with similar cases. Hondo and I faded into the background as the klieg lights went on and the reporters rushed to greet Rosemary and Hossi.

The senator, all smiles, picked Hossi up under his armpits and displayed him like a trophy. He hugged the kid. What a bunch of crap. Hossi promptly bit him on the nose.

Hondo and I had thirteen dollars between us.

Welcome to America.

chapter five

I was broke. Istanbul had hurt me financially. In Las Vegas terms, it was a push; we'd spent the entire fifteen thousand dollars in expenses. I still owed Hondo thirty-five hundred dollars for his fee and I didn't expect to see it anytime soon from Rosemary. She was crying poverty and I believed her. In addition to all this, I had felt obligated to get Hasan deported and this had taken some pull. Bureaucratic wheels spin slowly but none slower than those at the Immigration and Naturalization Service. While I didn't have to bribe anyone, I did call in some favors and went for a few hundred dollars in "business lunches." My immigration contacts never ate in any fancier place than Arbee's, but when they knew I needed a favor, I wound up eating next to the ladies who lunch in the Four Seasons.

I couldn't believe the amount of money I was going through. The monthly nut for my kids' new schools was bleeding me. We had paid off all our major bills. I was at ground zero. It had to be uphill from here.

I was still getting calls regarding kidnapping cases but this time I kept my word to myself. I refused to get involved. Instead, I started handling standard investigative assignments. I called every lawyer I knew and offered my services. The jobs came in but they were mostly tedious and predictable. Infidelity cases abounded.

I always get a kick out of fictional private investigators on television who don't handle divorce cases. Without divorce work, the average real-life PI couldn't survive. They're the bread and butter of the industry, at least when you're starting out. And I was starting out.

Almost all these cases are the same. Either a husband or a wife would call me and tell me they suspected their spouse of cheating. I would mount a surveillance, catch the person in the act, and collect my fee; end of case. I offer this bit of advice to all those people who suspect a philandering spouse: If you have a gut feeling that your significant other is cheating, you're probably correct. Instinct is usually right on the money. If you're thinking of divorcing the person, hire a licensed private investigator to gather the evidence. You're going to need it in court. Judges cast a jaundiced eye on a "friend of the family" who volunteers to follow the errant spouse around. Spring for a few dollars and do it right the first time.

Anyway, I would sleepwalk through most of these cases. There aren't too many innovative cheaters out there who can come up with new and novel ways to avoid detection. I offer two, however, that gave me a run for my money (or should I say the client's money?).

The first case involved a restaurateur who was making a ton of money with the two upscale Italian eateries he owned in midtown Manhattan. The restaurants were right across the street from each other; so successful were they that one was opened just to catch the overflow from the other.

The owner was certain his new wife was cheating on him. My new client was a dapper, shorter, Italian gentleman with a heavy accent and a penchant for expensive double-breasted suits. He was fifty-five. His bride was twenty-two years his junior and a flaming redhead with a knockout body. She towered above him and had been a model, but at that time she was working in the publishing business.

I got a hefty retainer up front and was instructed to follow her to a publishers' convention in Boca Raton, Florida. Tough duty. I stayed at the same hotel and dogged her for four days. She was friendly with her coworkers but that seemed to be as far as it went. I even bribed a bellman to keep his eye on her at night and check her sheets in the morning. I had her husband call her at odd times during the night. She was always in her room. Nothing.

I flew on the same plane with her back to New York. Hubby sent a limo to pick her up at La Guardia. Straight home. Still, he was convinced she was playing around. He had no hard (or, for that matter, soft) evidence. It was just his gut feeling. I thought he was a pretty street-smart guy so I stuck with the case.

My client had given his young wife a brand-new Ferrari as a wedding present (*I* would have married him for that car). Occasionally she would say she was going shopping after work or to friends in New Jersey. She would take the car. I figured that if she was doing anything wrong, these trips would be a perfect time for her to do it.

I decided to follow her in my unobtrusive Chevy. This ought to be simple, I thought. I can't really lose her in Manhattan; too much traffic. The first day she roared out of the garage under her east side building like Mario Andretti. The rush hour had yet to begin and in a matter of minutes she was on the Queensboro Bridge heading to Queens. There was little or no traffic. She wove around cars like Gene Hackman in *The French Connection*. I thought I was back in Denmark trying to elude the cops. I lost her on the Queens side.

This went on for two weeks, about four trips. Each time she headed to Queens and I would lose her somewhere in Long Island City. My client was getting peeved. His bill was way over ten grand. Finally I wised up. Every time I lost her I would start the next surveillance at that spot. The leapfrog effect. Eventually (two more weeks) I tracked her to a pizzeria in Astoria. She was getting it on with some twenty-year-old pizza maker. Hubby was crushed and tossed her out. I still eat in his restaurants and he's still seeing younger women. The older he gets, the younger they get. I check them all out and most are in it for the money. Sad.

The other case is the kind of caper PIs tell each other about at conventions. Unbelievable but true.

Todt Hill is an exclusive area of Staten Island. I started picking up work there almost from the start, being a Staten Island resident and connected to some local lawyers. A very wealthy businessman (older) suspected his wife (younger) of cheating. What a shocker. He was in his fifties and looked older, she was in her thirties and looked younger. He was the quintessential nerd: skinny, balding, with bifocals as thick as bulletproof glass. He was a computer genius who'd built a multimillion-dollar software empire. Looking at him, I would have guessed he sold hearing aids over the phone. But he had money and therefore he had a beautiful trophy wife. She was blond and in dynamite shape, spending most of her time at a local health club.

I followed her for two months, which meant I joined the health club and got in the best shape of my life. I knew her schedule better than she did. Leave the house, go to the club, go home. Occasionally, she would meet her sister for lunch or dinner. Nothing else. She and my client would go out together on weekends. I know nuns that lead wilder lives. I reported faithfully to my client once a week.

Finally, after the two months, I recommended we cut the surveillance. I liked my client and thought he was wasting his money. He wouldn't hear of it. He insisted she was seeing someone. How did he know? He just knew. Remember what I said about instinct and gut feelings? I had one other alternative: the polygraph.

The polygraph, or lie detector, always proved to be a useful tool on The Job. With a competent examiner, the polygraph is a very valuable instrument. I decided to see how it worked in the private sector.

To my surprise, my client's wife readily agreed to take the test. He asked her during dinner. I wonder how the conversation went.

"Excuse me, sweetheart, could you pass the mashed

potatoes, and by the way, you cheating, miserable bitch, would you take a polygraph test so I can find out whose face you're curtsying on?"

In retrospect, I figured she didn't have much of a choice. Refuse to take it and she would be branded a cheater. Her husband had the power: money. Better to take a chance even if she was cheating.

I got a former lieutenant from The Job to administer the test. I've known Pat, the polygraphist, for years and he's the best in the business. He said he'd handled a lot of infidelity cases. What a way to make a living. But I guess for a thousand dollars a pop he had learned to live with it.

I took the client to lunch while the exam was in progress. His wife seemed calm as we were leaving. The test was conducted in the client's home. We got back to his house just as Pat was finishing up.

"What's the verdict?" I asked. Pat was packing up his equipment. My client looked like he was awaiting the weekly lottery drawing. The wife was nowhere in sight.

"You're my client," he said to me, "I'll report to you . . . in private." He looked at the husband. "Procedure." That usually explains everything. Something was up. We went into the den and Pat closed the door behind us.

"Well?" I said.

Pat sat down, loosened the knot on his tie, and unbuttoned his shirt. He looked like he needed a drink. "She's not seeing another guy."

"Well, that's good." I thought about it. "Another woman?"

"Nope." He smiled.

"What then? Who are you, Monty Hall? I'm running out of curtains."

"She's banging the dog. Can I get paid now?"

"Dog, what dog?" I'd been around criminals so long I thought she was doing it with a street guy called The Dog.

"They've got a German shepherd. The dog is doing her."

I thought I had heard everything. I guess I hadn't. Pat told me that the wife wasn't having sex with her husband. He was impotent, or at least he was 90 percent of the time. Rather than cheat on her husband she'd decided to take on the pooch. Man's best friend. Now I realized where my client's "gut feeling" was coming from. His inability to satisfy the missus led him automatically to believe she was playing around.

"She told you this!?" I was shocked. What the hell was there left in this world that could shock me?

"Wags, I've been doing this a long time," Pat said matter-of-factly. "After I ran the first chart, I knew something was wrong. I got her to confess. I do it with murderers all the time. This was a walk in the park. She loves her husband, that's the funny thing about it. She wouldn't cheat on him, at least not with a two-legged creature." He leaned toward me. "You trying to figure out what to tell your client?"

What I was trying to decide was which window I was going to leave by. I couldn't imagine facing my client with news like that. I decided to ask the expert. "You tell me."

"I mentioned that I do fidelity cases all the time," Pat said. "I can't imagine what sort of dysfunctional couple would have to resort to a polygraph to work out their problems. On the one hand, I resent being in the middle, on the other hand, the thousand isn't bad. So I act like a priest. I don't care if the cheating wife is banging the Seventh Fleet or the husband is screwing Mary Poppins. They're all innocent."

"That's it? You don't tell the truth?"

Pat got up. "Now you've got it. But I do one better. I get them together and embarrass the shit out of the client for having me do the test in the first place. Then I tell the client, 'Your spouse loves you, don't you feel like an idiot?' The one I let slide promises they'll be as pure as the driven slush. Works every time. At least it gives me time to get the hell out of the house." He gathered up his equipment. "Now watch a pro in action."

Pat talked to the client first, then got the wife in the room. They held hands on the couch like newlyweds. I had the urge to toss her a Frisbee. Pat was good with them. Maybe they made it. I never heard from the client again.

A few weeks later, I got a phone call from a reporter who worked for a national magazine. She wanted to do a story on me. The reporter said she had gotten a call from one of my former clients who said that I would make a good subject for a story on custodial-interference cases. She wouldn't tell me the name of the person who had recommended me. I talked with the reporter for two days in my home. I didn't get paid for the interview but took the sage advice of the wise Beau Dietl, who once said, "Any publicity is good publicity." He was right. About a month after the interview, I hit the mother lode and it was because of the magazine article.

A woman from Chicago whose millionaire husband

owned a string of shopping malls and other commercial real estate suspected her husband of cheating. She had seen the article in the magazine and called me because her husband was going to be traveling for a series of business meetings and she wanted him watched. The woman had a slight Spanish accent, very cultured and refined. Simple enough, but hubby only traveled by private jet, which he piloted. This was a guy who traveled alone, flying wherever business took him.

All the wife knew was that her husband was scheduled to fly to San Diego on business one day the following week. She had no idea where he was going after that and suspected he was meeting another woman. I asked why she suspected him.

"Because I found a piece of paper in his wallet that had the words Useppa Island written on it. We know no one on this Useppa Island. I do not even know where it is located."

I knew Useppa Island to be a wealthy resort and residential area located off Ft. Myers, Florida. "Is he scheduled to make any other stops?"

"I think Washington, D.C. Perhaps his girlfriend lives there and they are going to this island together. Can you follow him and report back to me? I don't really care how much you will charge, I just want to know if my suspicions are correct."

She didn't care how much I charged? Music to my ears. "To do this right we're going to need teams in Washington, San Diego, and Ft. Myers, plus a jet. Your husband decides to alter course in the air and we've got a problem."

"I understand. How much will you need for a retainer?"

I decided to go for the gold. "We'll need fifty thousand dollars." I wondered if she heard my voice crack. She didn't hesitate and promised to meet me in New York with the money in two days.

We met in the Carlyle Hotel, in Manhattan. She had a suite and was traveling alone. I was surprised to see a knockout brunette with pouty lips. She was in a leather dress that stopped way above the knee. If I were hubby, I would have had *her* watched. She was short, with shoulder-length hair. Her skin had never seen the sun. A few visits to the plastic surgeon had left her of indeterminate age, somewhere between thirty and death. She handed me a cashier's check for the full amount. We were in business.

I needed a total of eight operatives, including myself: two in San Diego, two each at Washington's two private airports, and two in Ft. Myers. I chose to be part of a team in Washington, figuring I would be needed on the ground and in communication with my people in case of a problem. Hondo was part of the San Diego team and would follow our target in a rented jet. I wondered if Armani made flight suits. He hesitated about taking the job until I mentioned that I had his thirty-five hundred from the Istanbul case. The other operatives were made up of retired detectives from The Job.

A day before the husband was scheduled to land in San Diego, all the teams were in place.

I reviewed my financial status. Each operative was costing me $500 a day, plus expenses. The jet, a Lear 35, cost $1,750 an hour, actual air time—no frequent-flyer miles. Ground time was $400 a day, landing fees $200. Uncle Sam got 10 percent in tax. Three days would cost me about $16,000 for the plane and about

$15,000 for the men. I couldn't believe I was able to charge the jet on my American Express card. Good thing I didn't leave home without it.

Our target landed in California at around nine A.M. on a Thursday. Hondo reported via cell phone that he'd spent two hours in a meeting in a downtown bank and was heading back to the airport. It was one P.M. Hondo also told me that Hubby hadn't filed a flight plan and was not required to do so until he was ready to leave. We had no idea where he was going. I was sitting at Signature Airport outside Washington in a rented car with three cell phones, all with open lines. This, too, was costing a hefty sum.

Finally, our target filed a flight plan to where I was sitting, Signature Airport, Washington, D.C. He was in the air shortly thereafter with Hondo and another operative tailing him at 30,000 feet. I told the other teams to stand down. We waited.

Six hours later he was on the ground. Our Lear was right behind him. He was met by a woman (not his wife) who arrived ten minutes before he did in a black Lincoln Town Car. She was blond and gorgeous. The target looked like a sixty-year-old rich guy, except for the fact that he was wearing one of those World War II pilot caps with the fifty-mission crush. He gave her one peck on the cheek and they departed in the Lincoln. She dropped him off at a town house in Georgetown. We decided to follow her. I told Hondo on the cell phone to rent a car and sit on the Georgetown town house.

The woman drove to an estate on an acre of land in Virginia. We could barely see the house from the road. I ran her license plate on a laptop computer. She was a married woman, age thirty-seven. Now I'm trying to figure out how we're going to watch the house without attracting attention. We were in a *very* exclusive neighborhood. I was sure the local cops did their jobs well and thought we might also have to contend with a private security force. We were challenged by a cop within two hours of setting up the surveillance.

I decided to be straight with him. I identified myself and told him we were working a divorce case. He was an old-timer and must have heard the same story many times before because all he did was run our license plate to make certain the car wasn't stolen. He even told us he would inform his relief that we were there in case the surveillance dragged on.

No one left the house for three days. Danny, the retired detective I was with, wasn't a complainer, but after three days of sitting in a Ford Escort we were beginning to get on each other's nerves. We would stay at the site until two in the morning, assume she was in for the night and go to a local motel for three hours' sleep. We were back by dawn. I spent my days trying to stay awake and peeing in the woods. Hondo followed the target to and from business meetings during that time. He didn't meet with any women other than for business. Finally, on the fourth day, there was movement.

Our blonde rolled out of her compound at six-thirty in the morning in the same Lincoln Town Car. Hondo advised that our target was leaving the town house at about the same time. They met at a hotel for breakfast in D.C. and conveniently sat in front of a picture window. I shot two rolls of film of them eating scrambled eggs. There was no intimacy or even the aforementioned cheek peck. After breakfast she dropped him back at the town house and she went back to her home in Virginia.

Another day of tedium. Hubby attended meetings and the blonde stayed home. I wondered how much longer the target would be in the country. I saw hours as dollar signs with wings. Every hour he did nothing cost thousands. How much money would the wife go for before she gave it up?

About five o'clock on the afternoon of the fourth day, a black stretch limousine passed us and turned into the blonde's private driveway. The driver helped the lady of the house load numerous suitcases into the car. Something was up.

I got Hondo on the cell phone. "Where are you?"

"Sitting in front of the town house. Numb nuts was out all day. He just got back. Nothing's going on."

"Well, I think a move is under way. Call the pilot and have him warm up the Lear or whatever they have to do to it." I told him about the limo. "You may be getting a visit."

Sure enough, the limo came by and picked up the target. They were on their way to Signature. Finally. I got everyone in place. The team sitting on the second airport had long since been reassigned to Hondo. All four men were on the Lear before the black limo got to the airport. For two hundred dollars, the guy who handled the husband's flight plan reported to us before the ink was dry.

"They're going to Ft. Myers," Hondo said. What a surprise. The two operatives in Florida were waiting for them. I told Hondo that once they landed in Ft. Myers, his end of the job was completed, the Florida crew would take over. Hondo and his men took the Lear back to New York without landing in Florida.

Danny and I were in a hotel room in D.C. waiting to hear from the team in Ft. Myers. Three hours later my cell phone rang.

"The fucking eagle has landed, and it's about goddamn time," Rocco, one of the retired detectives said. Another limo picked the couple up at the airport in Ft. Myers and drove them to Useppa Island.

Rocco's partner, Andy, made the next call. "Wags, they're on the island, but I don't think we can get on. There's a security gate here with an armed square badge on post."

"Andy, see if you can stop the limo on the way out. Slip the driver a few bucks and get an address where he dropped the target." Andy called back fifteen minutes later. He'd talked to the driver and for fifty bucks he'd drawn Andy a map. That was the good news. The bad news was that they weren't within camera range.

"There's buildings and trees between us and the condo they're in," Andy said. "Why don't we just sit here till they come out? I mean, it's evident what they're doing in there. The client'll be happy."

I knew Andy was right, but for fifty grand the guy's wife deserved pictures. "Can you talk to the guard on the gate?" They said they would give it a try.

"No good, Wags," Rocco said on the cell phone ten minutes later. "He's a retired Ft. Myers PD, scared shitless about losing his job and benefits. We even did the 'brother officer' bullshit. No go."

"You offer him anything?"

"Two hundred. Turned it down."

"How much you got, between you and Andy?" Everybody had a price. There was a few minutes of silence. I had given the Florida crew four thousand dollars for expenses.

"Twenty-five hundred and change," Rocco said.

"Give him two thousand." We didn't have time to go into collective bargaining. The client would pay for it anyway.

Rocco sighed. "I was planning on going to the dog track before we left."

"Believe me, I'm saving you money." He knew I was right.

The money worked. During the next three days, Rocco and Andy shot ten rolls of film. They even got some clear shots of the happy couple having sex on the terrace of the condo. After a while, enough was enough. I gave Rocco and Andy an extra two days down there with pay. I flew back to New York for a meeting with the client.

The target's wife wasn't shocked when she saw the pictures. We were in her suite at the Carlyle sipping single-malt scotch.

"If a divorce action comes of this, we're available to testify," I said.

She shook her head. "Oh, I don't want to divorce him, I just want to confront him and make his life miserable for a little while." She crossed her legs. "Perhaps have a little fling of my own." She smiled.

I got the hell out of there. I didn't need someone following *me* around.

My pager started vibrating in the car while I was driving home. My home number appeared in the little window. I hadn't been home in almost a week but I had called my wife every day. She knew I was on my way. I figured I was being given a grocery assignment.

I juggled toll money for the Verrazano-Narrows Bridge and a half-smoked Lucky while I punched the two-digit preset number on the mobile phone. I knew something was wrong as soon as I heard my wife, Pat, say hello.

"Jimmy, where are you?" She sounded breathless, scared.

I felt my stomach tighten. "Approaching the toll on the Staten Island side of the bridge. What's wrong?"

She sobbed. "It's Jimmy," she said, barely able to get my eldest son's name out, "he might have cancer."

My arms suddenly felt like lead weights. The tight feeling in my gut disappeared as quickly as it had arrived, replaced by a tingling that began at the base of my spine and ended at the top of my skull. I was no longer able to control the car. My fingers felt like hot dogs as I tried ineffectually to grip the wheel. I actually had to lean against the steering column and use my forearms to guide the car toward the side of the road. I felt so light-headed I wasn't certain if I was going to make it.

I must have cut off a dozen cars as my Buick came to rest on the shoulder of the road. The phone was on the floor, on the passenger side. I was barely able to hear the faint sound of my wife's voice as she called my name.

I was about to enter every parent's nightmare.

chapter six

Both my parents died of cancer. My dad was just retiring from The Job when he was diagnosed with lung
cancer. He died fifteen years ago. My mom passed
away from brain cancer right before *I* retired. I was
very close to my parents. My mom lingered for eight
weeks in my home, my dining room turned into a
makeshift hospital room. Toward the end I injected her
with morphine every four hours to relieve her hellish
pain. It was a nightmare seeing a vibrant woman
waste away before my eyes. The end was a blessing,
and my wife and kids were wonderful in helping me
care for my mother and handle my grief.

Now my son.

Jimmy was sixteen years old, six feet two and
weighing one-eighty. He had been losing weight,
about twenty pounds in two months. He was also
lethargic, way out of character for an outgoing, sports-
minded young man. In the beginning my wife and I
thought he had contracted some kind of bug; the flu

was running rampant in his school at that time. While I was in D.C. on the case of the jet-setting cheater, my wife had decided to take him to a doctor. She didn't tell me because she assumed it was just a bug he couldn't shake and she didn't want to upset me.

He was given a series of tests. The results were negative but the oncologist said that there were six more tests to be conducted to determine if Jimmy had cancer and where in his body it was located. The doctor said he had all the classic symptoms: night sweats, weight loss, etc. When I came home I was met by my boy sporting a seven-inch gash in his neck from where four lymph nodes were removed.

He looked like hell. I now realized why my wife called me in the car before I walked through the front door. In the one week I was gone he deteriorated tremendously. He was extremely gaunt. His eyes were sunken and his skin had a gray pallor. He was scared, very scared. Sixteen. Just a boy.

After my wife and I had a good cry, we got the other kids together and discussed Jimmy's condition as a family. It wasn't easy, but I was proud of my kids for the way they handled the news. They were fresh off helping me care for my mom and knew about cancer. Jennifer was thirteen, Patricia, nine. My stepdaughter, Susan, was in her mid-twenties and had not lived at home for a while. It was decided that we would go on living as we had been doing, Jimmy would continue to attend school, and the rest of the diagnostic tests would be conducted around his academic schedule. We would try to be as normal as possible.

In addition to the mental anguish of waiting for test results, I knew I would be needing a pile of cash. The public thinks that a city worker, particularly a cop or a fireman, has a great health plan. The reality is that we have one of the worst insurance plans in the country. It's true that when a cop retires he takes his insurance with him, but the policy itself comes nowhere near covering actual costs. For example, children of retired cops are not covered for prescriptions. Hospital stays are covered up to 80 percent, but diagnostic tests in hospitals not requiring overnight stays, or that could be conducted on an out-patient basis, are hardly reimbursable. Since all Jimmy's tests were to be conducted on an out-patient basis, I knew we were going to get hit with a whopping bill. I also wanted the best care for my son, and to get it I had to hustle up some money.

The Florida philanderer case put some money in the bank but that would be wiped out in a short period of time. I had a friend, a lieutenant whose wife was diagnosed with cancer. She survived, but after insurance reimbursements, he wound up in debt for over one hundred thousand dollars. I didn't want to be destitute, but I was determined to provide my son with the best possible treatment.

To the phone.

Since I'd retired from The Job I had realized the value of being able to hustle. The sense of security at the NYPD, with the steady paycheck, is a double-edged sword. A cop knows the check is there twice a month whether he captures Carlos the Jackal or sits on his ass and does nothing. Hard work or no work bring in the same money, unless a cop gets lucky enough to pass a civil-service promotion test. Sometimes it takes many years even for the best and the brightest to get anywhere in a job so huge the sheer numbers dwarf the standing armies of some countries. There's no such thing as instant gratification on the NYPD unless you're a thief. Not so ATC (After the Cops).

The harder you work, the more money you make. I was determined to get as much work in as little time as possible. And so, to the phone.

The Florida case was an anomaly. Normally, I work for other security professionals or private investigators. Private investigators run a particularly high risk of getting stiffed by clients. I've lost track of how many PIs have told me that they weren't paid by a client after following an alleged cheating spouse for weeks only to find out they weren't cheating. Instead of being pleased that their significant other wasn't playing around, the client would be pissed that after spending thousands they didn't have a cheater to show for it. I decided I'd much rather work for a licensed PI. You always get paid, not because the business is littered with honest people but because it's a small industry and getting a reputation as someone who doesn't pay the help will put a PI out of business before you can say Maltese falcon.

I put the word out to a dozen PIs that I was looking for work, anything quasi-honest that paid well and quickly. I expected to wait a day or two for a return call and was pleasantly surprised when a Manhattan investigator, McCoy Paz, called me back within fifteen minutes. He had a client who needed a bodyguard.

"She's a rich dame, needs company more than security." Shades of the Arabs, I thought. "A real cushy assignment. She's an heir to a computer software fortune." He mentioned the company. A household name. "Likes to come to New York the first week of the month to do the social scene. Late forties, plenty of cash. All you gotta do is take her around, make sure she doesn't get mugged and gets into the good restaurants. She'll be in for at least a week. Great job, pays good."

"How good?"

"Seven-fifty a day, plus expenses."

"When do I start?"

He paused. "Could you be at the Plaza in two hours? When she's back at the hotel, you're free to go, just show up the next day whenever she needs you."

Such a great assignment and he hadn't found anyone to handle it up until now? I smelled a rat but I couldn't bring myself to question the job. "She travel alone?"

"Oh, yeah." I was to find out why very shortly.

My son was scheduled to undergo another diagnostic test the following day, and while I didn't want to leave his side, my wife convinced me that he would be going to bed shortly and I would be back in plenty of time to be there when he woke up. My wife would accompany him to the test.

I quickly showered. By the time I was ready to leave the house, Jimmy was asleep. I went to his bedside. He was bundled under a comforter and looked like the little boy I had read to when he was three. The tears flowed as I brushed back his hair, the urge to crawl in bed next to him overwhelming. When he was a little kid, he would have the occasional nightmare and he would call for his daddy in the middle of the night. When I would enter his room, he would be standing in the middle of the bed holding a stuffed Pooh, somewhere in the netherworld between sleep and consciousness. I would tuck him in and lie down next to him, unwilling to leave until I knew he was back in a kid's world of dreams and security. My little boy. Only a parent could know the anguish.

I was standing in the lobby of the Plaza Hotel after the desk clerk informed me that my client would be down shortly. He mumbled, "Good luck," under his breath. I began to wonder what I had gotten myself into. Having no idea where we would be going I wore my most neutral suit, a navy blue, double-breasted Brioni, white shirt, red patterned silk tie, and gleaming black Ballys. I was ready for either a funeral or to testify in front of a grand jury.

"You Wigs?"

I turned. "Wags," I said. If this was my client and she was in her forties, I was eleven. She appeared to be at least sixty, with a mane of disheveled jet-black hair haphazardly piled on her head. A dye job from a bottle of industrial-strength liquid shoe polish. The hair had been spray-painted with some kind of lacquer that a bullet couldn't penetrate. Her face was pinched and well-lined, festooned with enough broken veins to accurately double for a relief map of Georgia. She wore sunglasses and I was spared looking at her eyes. Her body looked like a collapsed soufflé. She was extremely thin, and dressed in a pants suit big enough to fit Ethel Merman. And oh, yes, she had a parrot on her shoulder.

"It's Wags," I repeated, gawking at the huge multicolored bird.

"Whatever," she said. She reeked of alcohol and was quite loaded. "I'm Grace." She extended her hand. I took it. The bird squawked.

Her hand came off!

I stared down in disbelief. I was holding the

woman's right hand in mine. She was cackling like a witch, hysterical to the point where she began hacking a powerful smoker's cough.

The goddamn hand felt real. The fingers were adorned with two rings. A gold Rolex watch dangled on three inches of wrist.

I muttered, "What the fuck?" I didn't know what to do with the hand. I looked at where the hand should be and saw an empty sleeve. A bellman breezed by and whispered out of the side of his mouth, "You've been officially greeted by Grace-from-Outer-Space. Good luck, you're gonna need it."

My client finally calmed down and grabbed the hand with the one she had left. She screwed it into her sleeve. It stayed. "Come on, honey," she rasped, "I'm thirsty." She grabbed my arm and led me toward the revolving door. The parrot took a nip at my ear. I broke loose and changed sides.

"Don't mind Johnson. He won't hurt you, he just doesn't like men." I felt every eye in the lobby staring at us.

A black super-stretch limo was parked out front. A uniformed chauffeur already had the door open. "Evening, ma'am," he said.

"Hi, Ralph." She pointed to me. "This is Wigs."

"Wags," I corrected. Grace got in the car. Ralph extended his hand. I hesitated.

"It's real. I guess you've been welcomed." He cocked his head toward Grace. Ralph was about fifty with a stomach that strained at his jacket. We shook hands.

"Can I talk to you for a second?" I said. Grace was already at the bar, clunking ice in a mixing tumbler.

Ralph closed the door gently. We moved toward the back of the car. "This broad sane?" I asked.

Ralph smirked. "She's rich, so she ain't crazy, she's eccentric. I'm the only driver'll take her around. The other guys can't put up with her bullshit."

"Why do you?"

He rubbed three fingers together. "I got four kids. She tips good." I asked about the hand.

"She lost it when she was a kid. Never asked how." We broke it off. I joined Grace in the back. She was using the mixing tumbler as a cocktail glass. There were three cubes floating around in at least a pint of vodka. The bird was eyeing me like an eagle.

She yelled at Ralph, "Let's go to the China Club."

"It's a little early for that, ma'am, maybe you want some dinner?"

I got the impression that Ralph was trying to take care of his passenger. She looked like she rarely ate. She looked at me. "You hungry?"

I'd rather see her eating than tossing down drinks in some club. "Yeah, sure."

"Okay, Ralph," she slurred, "take us to Dock's." Johnson screeched. I guess he was hungry. Grace lit a cigarette. She would do two packs before the end of the night.

The popular seafood restaurant on Broadway was packed. Grace jammed a pile of bills in my pocket and told me to get us a table. I gave a guy in a suit ten bucks and we were seated within two minutes. Even the most jaded New Yorkers couldn't keep their eyes off the bird.

We weren't settled three minutes when Grace started getting belligerent.

"Where's the fucking waiter?" People at adjoining tables turned to look at her. Or was it the bird?

"Look, Ms.—" I kept my voice low. I embarrass easily.

"Call me Grace."

"Okay . . . Grace," I said. "We just got here, the place is jammed. Let's give them a few minutes." I gave her a friendly smile, hoping it would mollify her.

She looked at me like I was an idiot.

Then she unscrewed her hand.

"Service over here!" She had a voice like Broderick Crawford. One waiter turned to respond but apparently wasn't fast enough because she began to bang her prosthesis on the table. Khrushchev would have been proud. "I want a fucking drink!"

To this day I can't figure out why we weren't thrown out of there. Apparently, the owner knew her because he ran over and tried to calm her down. Maybe he took pity on her. He sweet-talked Grace while I snatched the hand away from her. She didn't seem to notice. Now I'm sitting in a respectable restaurant holding a hand. I wanted to smack her across the face with it but felt that would be poor public relations. Instead, I put it under my jacket and hoped the goddamn thing wouldn't come to life and tickle me.

Somehow we made it through dinner. Grace had five Belvedere vodkas on the rocks. She had asked for martinis with no vermouth or olives. She ordered a lobster, which I ended up eating. Kind of difficult to cut up lobster with one hand. All she was concerned about was how quickly the waiter could fetch the next vodka. Thank God there were no more outbursts. The check came to $154. She left a $100 tip. On the way out the door I could swear I heard the entire staff let out the breath they had been collectively holding for the last ninety minutes.

As we entered the limo, I gave Grace the prosthesis. "I think this is yours."

She screwed it back into the sleeve, only the palm wound up facing up. I didn't say anything. At least she could tell us when it started to rain.

We had been in the China Club for twenty minutes when the fight broke out. I was just coming out of the men's room when I saw a bunch of people on the floor. Actually, it was three bouncers trying to pry Grace off the back of a forty-year-old stockbroker type. Grace was beating him over the head with her phony hand and yelling at the top of her lungs.

"You motherfucker! Reagan was a fucking thief just like the rest of you fucking Republicans!" Her jacket was ripped up the back seam and she had lost a shoe. Her parrot was sitting on the bar taking it all in. The man she was hitting was bleeding from the nose and was shielding his face. She definitely had the upper hand, no pun intended. I jumped into the melee and for my trouble was punched in the head by a bouncer. It took me a good two minutes to calm everyone down. We were shown the door.

"And stay the fuck out," were the last words I heard as the door slammed behind us. My head throbbed. Ralph was leaning against the car, grinning. Suddenly I envied him. I wondered if he would like to switch jobs. I tried to help Grace into the car but she shook off my assistance. The parrot bumped his head on the roof.

"I was winning the goddamn fight! Why'd you have to bust it up?" She looked like hell. She had taken a nasty scratch over her left eye and her hair was sticking up at every angle imaginable. She looked like Don King.

I shoved her in a seat. "Lady, I quit. Keep your goddamn money and drop me off at the hotel. The night is young, have a good time." The way I felt, I'd sooner drink toxic waste than put in another minute with that psycho.

She looked at me and smiled. Her teeth were stained the color of tree bark. "Aw, c'mon, I'll be good. Tell you what, I'll give you a raise. How much you making?"

I told her. I couldn't figure out why she needed me, or anyone else, for that matter.

"I'll double it."

How much worse could it get? Maybe she was so shit-faced she just lost control. If I continued this job, I'd have to try to limit her booze intake. "No more fights?"

She shook her head like a scolded child.

"No more taking off that thing?" I pointed to the hand. Another head shake. Fifteen hundred bucks. Every man has a price. "Okay."

She agreed to go back to the hotel. She would have stayed out longer but the scratch on her head was still bleeding and she was concerned about her appearance. This from a woman whose jacket was covered with bird shit.

Grace settled down in the car with another drink. The bird sat stoically on her shoulder. I could tell he had been through this before.

Grace leaned on my arm because she couldn't navigate the hotel lobby without falling. I damn near pushed her into the room. She staggered three steps and collapsed on the bed, feet dangling on the floor. I straightened her out and propped a pillow under her head. She belched. The end to a perfect night.

I made two phone calls from the lobby. The first was to my wife. Jimmy still slept peacefully. Pat was going into his room every half hour to check on him. I couldn't wait to get home. I wanted my face to be the first thing he saw when he woke up. He hadn't been able to do that lately.

The second call was to McCoy Paz. It was a little after one A.M. and I got great pleasure out of waking him up. It took him a good half minute to shake the sleep off.

"Hey, Mac," I said in my most grating voice, "why didn't you tell me I'm dealing with a lunatic?" I recounted the battle in the China Club.

"Listen, Wags, I'm sorry. I couldn't get anyone to watch the broad. All my regulars begged off, they've dealt with her before."

"You couldn't get anyone for seven-fifty a day?"

"Nobody who wouldn't start drinking with her and stealing her money. I got my license to worry about."

I'm glad he thought I was honest. Stupid, but honest. "Why the hell does she need security anyway?" I heard the distinctive snap of a Zippo lighter. I needed a smoke too.

"It's a condition of her allowance. She's the black sheep of the family." What a surprise. "Her people make like she doesn't exist but give her a regular stipend. The family requires she have security to keep her out of trouble. No security, no money. You ain't quitting, are you?" He sounded desperate. "I clear two large a week from her. I'll raise you to a grand a day."

I told him about my new salary.

"She better be payin' it out of her own pocket."

I told Mac I'd stick with it without telling him why I needed the money. He told me he owed me one and I let him get back to sleep. Sleep seemed like a pretty good idea.

Grace was a night person. Another shock. I was on my beeper the next day and didn't hear from her or Mac. I was able to go to the hospital with Jimmy and my wife. They conducted a test that lasted two hours, the results of which we would get in one day. Poor kid, he looked drained. I actually got to go home and have dinner with my family. Paz called at seven P.M. I was being summoned.

Same deal. Same bird. Different outfit. That night she was wearing a short pleated skirt, white sweater, and black suede vest. The black spike heels she wore accentuated her scrawny legs. She had her hair down. The parrot was naked, like the previous night.

"Hiya, Wigs."

I didn't correct her. I wondered if she remembered anything that had happened the night before. She was loaded again. Vodka doesn't have an odor but she was navigating the Plaza lobby like she was avoiding incoming artillery. Ralph was back at his post in the limo.

She was very talkative in the car. That worried me. I suspected cocaine, a lot of it. She told me she was *forty* years old. When I appeared skeptical, she showed me a Michigan driver's license. I pictured her house, full of Kewpie-dolls, won at guess-your-age stands at carnivals. A prime candidate for an alcohol-abuse ad campaign. I know I vowed to cut back.

Our first stop was the Mark Hotel for dinner. The Mark is a very stiff, upscale hotel that has one of the city's finest restaurants. It cost her a C note to get the bird admitted, with a caveat. The parrot had to be *seated* with us. She couldn't wear him. Good news for her dry cleaners. She acted normal for the first five minutes, probably because her first drink arrived expeditiously. She ordered her second drink by throwing an ashtray at a waiter. We were thrown out immediately. I was mortified.

She started doing lines of coke in the limo. She'd do a line and have a blast of vodka right from the bottle. I thought, Screw it, and I joined her. Not in the drugs, just the booze. We drove around Manhattan for an hour. She was getting paranoid and was convinced someone was following us. Every minute she would look out the back window and have Ralph take evasive action. I was starting to get carsick.

She threw a shoe at Ralph. "Take me to the Delmonico Hotel."

"What for?" I asked.

"I'm staying there tonight. They'll never suspect I changed hotels."

"Makes sense to me." I had another drink. Grace took *five* rooms at the Delmonico. She wanted to confuse the enemy. The rooms cost $650 each. When she'd finished registering, she got back in the limo.

"We're going to Connecticut."

Why the hell not? Her rationale was that the people who were following her would never figure her for Connecticut, not with five rooms at the Delmonico and one at the Plaza.

She had a definite destination in mind, a bed and breakfast in Fairfield. She had to own it, I couldn't see anyone admitting her to a psycho ward, let alone a tranquil B and B.

Grace began getting amorous in the car. She was horny. She dropped a hint very subtly.

"I want to suck your dick."

"That's nice," I said, "but I don't think so."

"Why not? I'll pay you."

"I'm married." That, and the fact that even in my wildest single days, when I was twenty and had testosterone flowing like the Colorado River, would I ever consider doing anything with Grace. A regular Bo Derelict. After a while she was convinced I would have nothing to do with her and she went back to her coke and vodka, two of the four food groups.

The owner of the B and B knew her. She had obviously done this before. I'm sure she paid at least triple the going rate. She got the last room. Ralph slept on a couch, I slept in the car. I think I got the better end of the deal.

We followed the same basic schedule for the rest of the week. Even the parrot was getting peeved. We were thrown out of the best restaurants and bars in New York. She damaged a bar on the east side to the tune of seven thousand dollars. I turned my back on her for a minute and she tossed a chair through a mirror and wiped out the top shelf of the bar with two ashtrays.

Through all this my family was still weathering Jimmy's tests. He had taken four so far and they were all negative. Still, he continued losing weight and had virtually no appetite. He was scheduled to take three more tests, including another type of biopsy.

At least Grace occasionally took my mind off Jimmy. We almost got arrested in Connecticut. The word was getting around in New York. Bouncers and doormen would see us coming and either lock the doors or refuse to admit us. She was a woman without a gin-mill. She had to go to another state to get a drink.

So we're on some back road in Connecticut in a tiny bar filled with retired telephone company workers. Grace was ripped on vodka and coke. Why should today be different than any other? Out of the blue she hits some old man over the head with a glass. They wind up rolling around on the floor, the bird sandwiched between them. State police come. We get hauled away. It took all my persuasive "brothers in blue" bullshit to get us out of there. We were banned from the entire state! I had had enough. I quit. Screw the money.

Two weeks later I got a phone call from Grace. She sounded only half drunk. She had called to apologize for her behavior. She felt so bad because of the way she'd acted she'd decided to throw a party. I was the guest of honor. I could bring whomever I wanted. The bash was to be held at a ski resort in Michigan.

"Please say you'll come."

"Wild horses couldn't keep me away." I would sooner slam a toilet seat on my penis. "How many people can I bring?"

"Five . . . no, ten. Bring ten people." She was paying for everything—airfare, hotel, food, booze, and anything else we wanted.

I've got a sick kid at home and a family that needs me. I signed on as security, nothing else. While I felt sorry for the lady, I wanted nothing to do with her or her parties. She'd be so bombed she wouldn't know if I was there or not. I think she just wanted company. The next day I faxed her a list of ten of my friends and people I worked with who said they wanted to go. Hondo went; so did Frank and Tony from the Arab job.

The other "guests" were divorced or retired cops who had nothing better to do. What the hell, it was a freebie.

I called Hondo when he got back.

"Have a good time?" I asked.

"I don't remember."

That said it all.

Grace calls occasionally when she's in town. I can't believe she's still alive. Someone has to be "guarding" her. I'm just glad it's not me.

chapter seven

My son's condition continued to worsen. It was now an effort for him to get out of bed in the morning. During the week I was back, he lost another seven pounds. He was into his third week of tests. The poor kid was getting poked and prodded on an almost daily basis and he never complained. Every test came back negative. For a while it was thought that he had chronic fatigue syndrome. Negative. The oncologist said that while the negative results were promising, they still didn't mean that Jimmy was cancer-free. All the indications were that he had the dreaded illness. I spent all the time I could with him, accepting only jobs that paid very well or were favors for people I worked with.

After another week of brain scans, an MRI, a GI series, and several other tests I couldn't pronounce, the doctor told my wife and me that if the last test, a lymph-node biopsy, came out negative, then my son didn't have cancer. Naturally we prayed for the right results, but in the back of my mind I wondered that if he didn't have cancer, what the hell did he have? The biopsy was scheduled for a Monday. We had three days to wait. It was torture but not nearly as torturous as the two days of nail-biting stress we had to endure waiting for the results.

While we waited it out, I got a call from a PI on Long Island who had a problem he wouldn't discuss on the phone. I went to his office. Whitey Anderson was a retired Nassau County detective who ran a small PI business just outside New York City. I knew Whitey from when I had made an off-duty arrest in Nassau many years before. We stayed in touch. Actually, his business wasn't small, it was minuscule. He had three clients, one of whom was a very well-known Broadway producer. Of Whitey's three clients, the producer was his bread and butter. The producer had a problem.

"He's being blackmailed," Whitey said.

"You know who's doing it?" I asked. I was seated in Whitey's office, which was located in his house—in the basement, actually. Whitey's office decor consisted of a battered desk situated next to a refrigerator. Low overhead.

"Oh, yeah, his former boyfriend. He's threatening to expose the producer as gay."

"This is the nineties, who cares who's gay anymore?"

"I think maybe my client's wife and kids might be concerned," Whitey said. "He's been in the closet all his life."

I knew as much about Whitey's client as the rest of the general public. He was a high-profile celebrity. I had never given his sexual orientation any thought, but he certainly didn't look gay. But then again, neither does Clint Eastwood. Just kidding.

I was a little more than puzzled. "What do you need me for?" Whitey was more than capable of handling a run-of-the-mill blackmail case. Regarded as an intellectual, Whitey could outthink Henry Kissinger.

"The boyfriend's not budging. He's outwardly homosexual, no skeletons. He wants fifty thousand dollars from my client or he starts making phone calls. You and I know it won't be the last bite."

"Try recording your conversation with him?"

Whitey nodded. "Our blackmailer insists on calling the fifty grand a loan. There's nothing on the tape that will compromise him. I think I need muscle."

I was a little surprised that Whitey thought of me as a strong-arm guy.

"I know what you're thinking, Wags. I don't mean *real* muscle. I mean the *appearance* of muscle. I obviously don't fit the bill."

An understatement if there ever was one. Whitey just about made the five-foot-eight height requirement for The Job. I think he had to hang by his thumbs for a week to do it. He couldn't have weighed more than 150 pounds. Whitey was always the cop they used when kids had to be interviewed. Enough said.

I, on the other hand, scare myself when I get up in the morning. In addition to my height, I've been lifting weights most of my life and come in at well over two hundred pounds. All solid. My face has been compared to Robert Urich's after a hunting accident. I've got most of my hair, a prerequisite for a bad-guy image. Could you imagine Jason Alexander intimidating anyone? While I'm not the violent type, I could see me scaring the hell out of someone. Show me a cop who isn't a good actor and I'll show you a dead cop.

We worked out the details. The blackmailer was an interior decorator (another shocker) who lived in Baltimore. Because Whitey was on a budget, I was to take a train to Baltimore, cab it to the guy's house and proceed to scare the shit out of him, then come back. The whole thing would take maybe eight hours.

"How's seven-fifty sound?" Whitey asked. "My client's a cheap bastard."

It sounded like a nice, easy job. "Count me in."

I drove home, put on my black silk Cerruti suit, white-on-white seal-cotton shirt, pearl gray tie, and black Ferragamos. A matching pocket silk completed my look.

"Who're you supposed to be, John Gotti?" my wife asked. I had passed the test.

The train ride took three hours. I tried to get lost in a book but my mind kept wandering to my son. One more day and we would know the answer. I was beginning to lose weight from worrying, my usual big appetite replaced by a gnawing in my gut that couldn't be mistaken for hunger. The bags under my eyes went well with my new look.

It was a short trip by taxi from the train station to the blackmailer's house. His decorating business must have been doing well because the house was located in a very exclusive gated community. A ten spot reserved my cab. I flipped the rent-a-cop my duplicate shield to gain entrance.

The doorbell chimed with the first few notes of "One," from *A Chorus Line*. The man who answered the door was about thirty, tall, thin, and dressed in leather pants, a white silk shirt, and no shoes. I looked for a button that read "stereotype."

"You Kevin Jacobson?" I asked in my toughest voice. I had been practicing on the train.

"Yes." He looked me up and down.

"Your former boyfriend has something for you."

He looked confused. "Former boyfriend?"

I mentioned his ex-lover's name.

"Oh, really, and what might that be?" He smiled and looked at my hands. I think he was expecting an envelope stuffed with money.

I slapped him across the face with an open palm. This was a spur-of-the-moment decision. I had to weigh trying, like a Dutch uncle, to talk some sense into the guy—which might take some time—or using whatever means necessary so I could catch the four o'clock train back to New York and see my son before he went to bed. Not much of a dilemma.

The slap couldn't have scattered the bubbles in a bathtub but Jacobson acted like he'd been hit in the face by a Louisville Slugger.

"Oh, my God, you hit me!" he squealed as he retreated a few steps. He was holding the side of his face. Tears welled in his eyes.

I took a giant step inside and slammed the door behind me. Jacobson cowered. He tucked his head behind his forearms. I grabbed him by his hair. It felt like a greasy chicken. I didn't want to be caught with a gun in another state so I had brought a mean-looking double-action switchblade knife with me. If I was searched, the knife would appear to be the ordinary legal pocket variety, but there was a hidden button under the pocket clip that activated a spring and made it a switchblade. The blade snapped open with authority. Jacobson's eyes went wide. He began to blubber. I put the blade under his chin.

"I understand you no longer wish to take a loan from your friend, is that right?" My voice was reasonable and calm. I had once heard Richard Widmark say the same line, or close to it, in a movie. I do a better DeNiro, but I didn't think calling Jacobson a "Mook" would necessarily scare him.

"No! No! No!" Jacobson was slobbering. He actually peed in his pants. I was beginning to feel sorry for the guy. "I swear, no money! I'll give *you* money! Please don't kill me!"

I pushed him on his ass. He was on his back, propped up by his elbows. I folded the knife and put it in my pocket. I gave him one of my bad-guy looks. "Call him once more, even if it's to wish him a happy birthday, and *I'll be back*!" Arnold would have been proud.

I left him curled in the fetal position. My taxi was waiting; I was back on the train within thirty minutes.

It was dusk by the time I retrieved my car from a garage by Penn Station in Manhattan. For some reason, I was calm, almost serene. My son's final test results were coming in the next morning and for the past week I'd been wound tighter than a coiled spring. The sun was setting beyond the Verrazano-Narrows Bridge as I cruised up to the toll booth. I was two miles from my house but I decided to go in another direction.

I've never been a religious person. When I was a kid, I was an altar boy but only because my parents thought it was a good idea. To me, St. Ann's was just another place to have a good time. I was always getting into some sort of trouble and the priest would invariably have to call my mom. I remember one day when my friend Georgie Iafe and I were to serve benediction after the eleven A.M. Sunday services. I was probably about ten years old. It was our job to march to the altar holding lit candles and looking somber.

Since we had some time to kill, we thought it would be a good idea to melt some candles and wax my eyes shut. Just when the job was done, an altar boy came into the sacristy and gave us our cue. We were on! I managed to get one eye cleared but didn't have time to get the wax off the other one. I served benediction with one eye waxed shut. The priest didn't think it was funny but Georgie and I thought it was hysterical. I was grounded for a week.

I hadn't been to church other than for funerals and weddings since I was a teenager. But that day I felt the need to pray. I just *knew* it was going to do some good.

The church was exactly the same. Nothing was changed, not even the unlocked poor box. I think that to add some order to our lives it's a rule that churches not be modified. We *expect* them to look exactly the same. To make cosmetic improvements would be blasphemy.

I talked to God that night. I asked him to spare my son. A simple request, I thought. I wasn't asking anything for myself, I just wanted him to live. I was there for maybe twenty minutes. During that time not one other person came inside. I guess everybody else's kids were in good shape.

By the time I got home, Jimmy was asleep. The two girls were in bed shortly thereafter. It was a school night. My wife and I stayed up and talked. We looked at half a dozen family photo albums and saw our kids grow up on glossy three by fives. We killed a bottle of white wine and went to bed holding each other. We were drained.

Jimmy bounded down the stairs the next morning like he had just won the lottery. He still looked like a skeleton, but the color was back in his cheeks and we saw him smile for the first time in weeks. My wife and I were a little shocked and didn't say anything, fearing that his mood change was just manic and he would crash at any time. But it didn't happen.

The doctor's appointment was scheduled for early afternoon. Jimmy naturally took off from school and my wife and I spent the morning with him giggling at stupid talk shows on television and snacking on junk food. He had regained some of his appetite.

We were thirty minutes early getting to the doctor's office. The three of us were sitting in his waiting room like kids anticipating a visit to the principal. The nurse led us into the office, right on time. The doctor was seated at his desk, head buried in a manila folder. He looked up and smiled.

Negative! Our son was cancer-free.

My wife and I burst into tears. We hugged our son, who sat starry-eyed, on the verge of hyperventilating.

As far as the doctor could tell, there was nothing wrong with Jimmy. That was the good news. The bad news—if you could call it that—was that we still didn't know why Jimmy was experiencing his symptoms. We left the office after being advised by the doctor to take a wait-and-see approach. We would monitor Jimmy's weight and return to the office in two weeks for reevaluation. The doctor was straight with us. Our son had been given every test known to the medical profession.

The doctor was stumped, and so were the doctors with whom he had consulted.

We got back in the car and headed home, our euphoria tempered by fear of the unknown. I reached over the seat to give Jimmy a high five.

"You know, Dad, I knew the test was going to be negative."

My wife said, "What do you mean you *knew*?"

I watched my son in the rearview mirror. He shook his head. "I just *knew*. I woke up last night and felt a presence in my room; I didn't see anyone, I just *felt* this . . . thing." Our eyes locked in the mirror.

"What time was that?" I asked.

Jimmy looked at me strangely. "I don't know . . . I think right after I went to bed. It didn't seem like I was in the room very long."

Right about the time I was in church.

He leaned against the front seat and continued. "I heard a voice, like it was coming from inside my head, I swear to God, Dad. This voice, it said, 'Don't worry, everything's going to be just fine.' And I believed it, Dad, it sounded so . . . like, comforting." He seemed to be groping for words. "I just knew . . . I just knew." He collapsed back into his seat. He seemed tired. "I remember rolling over on my side and smiling. I went to sleep. When I got up this morning, nothing bothered me. I really felt good, for the first time in, like, weeks."

From that day on, he steadily improved. It took him about six months to regain the weight he had lost. Today, three years later, he's in perfect health, the only reminder of his illness the seven-inch scar on his neck from the first biopsy. We never found out why he suffered the symptoms he battled for those few months.

Do I believe my trip to church had anything to do

with what I consider my son's miraculous recovery? It's hard to say. Cops, in general, are cynical people. Just because I had been retired a few years didn't make me any less a cop. Cops, as a whole, see too much suffering to make them true believers. But, if I was a total cynic, I'd be sticking up banks. More than one positive thing came from Jimmy's illness. I make it back to St. Ann's every now and then.

chapter eight

My family and I were thrilled by Jimmy's miraculous recovery. There's nothing like the threat of a catastrophic illness to bring a family closer together. We are a tight-knit family to begin with, and the cancer scare bonded us like Siamese sextuplets. The euphoria died down when the bills started trickling in. I didn't feel the frantic need to horde huge sums of money, however; I just went back to work. Jimmy was alive; we'd pay the damn bills eventually.

More traditional private investigations were coming my way. One of the first cases I became involved with after Jimmy's illness concerned an accused arsonist I'll call Abe Markowitz. Abe, it seems, was suspected of burning down his house to collect the insurance money. He hired a very well-known Manhattan attorney to represent him against the insurance company, which was refusing to pay the claim. The attorney hired me to make sure his client was telling him the truth when he said he was innocent. There's nothing more embarrassing for a lawyer than to go to court and get a nasty surprise, in this case an eight-by-ten glossy of Abe lighting a match under his porch, or something equally incriminating.

I did a routine investigation and couldn't ascertain one way or the other if Abe was guilty or innocent. He had some financial problems, but who doesn't? There was nothing criminal in his background to suggest he would be the type to defraud an insurance company. He ran a moderately successful small business. He didn't associate with anyone called "The Torch," which is always a good sign.

Abe's lawyer decided to polygraph his client. The lawyer realized that if I couldn't come up with anything to incriminate his client, then neither could the insurance company. If Abe could pass a polygraph test, the attorney would volunteer Abe to take a test administered by the insurance company. If Abe failed his attorney's test, then the results would be shit-canned—excuse me—discarded, and no one would be the wiser.

I got my friend Pat, the retired lieutenant who tested the dog lover on Staten Island, to test Abe. The examination was conducted in the attorney's office. I waited for the results, along with the lawyer, in a saloon across from city hall. I got beeped, summoning us back to the office after about two hours.

"Lying like a rug," Pat said as he packed up his equipment. Pat, it seemed, had managed to get a half-assed confession out of Abe. "He said he *may* have accidentally spilled some cleaning fluid in his basement while he was shampooing the carpet."

"So how'd the place go up?" the attorney asked.

Pat smiled. "He *may* have dropped some cigar ashes on the cleaning fluid."

"I *may* kick him square in the nuts," the lawyer said. Lawyers can lie; no one else can.

Abe and the lawyer wound up regrouping and sticking to their guns. Eventually Abe persevered and collected a few hundred thousand from the insurance company. I figured I had heard the last of Abe. Not so.

About six months later, Abe called me. He said he had something important to discuss with me that he couldn't mention over the phone. We set up a meeting in a restaurant in Little Italy. I made sure I brought my gun. Hey, you never know.

Abe was about forty years old, stocky, with a head of thick black hair just beginning to go salt and pepper. He was seated in the rear of the small, empty Italian restaurant with his back to the door. It was two in the afternoon; we had missed the lunch crowd. Abe was easy to spot. I slid into the seat opposite him, which commanded a full view of the door. At least I wasn't going to get assassinated. The mandatory small talk followed. Yes, I was fine; yes, he was fine, everybody felt great. We ordered lunch.

"I got a business deal for you," he finally said after extolling the virtues of the clam sauce.

"What, we gonna open up a 'Firebugs R Us'?"

"Very funny." He smiled through clenched teeth. "This is a real deal. You ever hear of the super carrier program?" I shook my head. "You know about the problems some airlines are having with drugs?"

"Why don't you tell me?"

Some airlines, he said, particularly the carriers that flew the Caribbean–South American route, were getting busted in record numbers because some of their aircraft were found to have drugs hidden in them. U.S. Customs would routinely levy huge fines against the offending airlines, and in some cases seize entire planes, even though the airline itself was not held criminally responsible.

"It's usually the employees," Abe said. "A flight attendant will get a few grand to smuggle in some coke, say a key or two. Sometimes it's marijuana. They hide the stash on the plane and try to come back for it or have someone else pick it up. They stick it everywhere; the johns, the wheel wells, every goddamn place you could think of. Customs comes with the drug dogs, finds the shit, confiscates it, and slaps the airline with a heavy fine."

I thought he was going to say he had come up with a foolproof method for smuggling drugs.

He leaned across the table. "I got this uncle, he's a retired army general. He comes up with this idea. What if he can convince customs that the airlines can police their own industry? What if the airlines search *their own* planes and turn over the shit they find? Would customs go easier on them?"

A lot of "what ifs," I thought.

"Well, it worked," Abe said. "The General struck a deal with customs." His uncle would always be referred to as "the General." It was kind of cute. I thought about calling *my* uncle "the Bus Driver." Abe speared a lone piece of ziti. "We're already working on getting personnel."

The super carrier program was created. It took a year to put it together. Customs would allow the airlines to police themselves to help mitigate their fines. Here's how it worked: Customs would still get first crack at the planes. Airlines in the program would get three "passes." If a fourth load was found, the heavy fines would resume. After the initial search, security hired by the airline would conduct a *second* search. If *they* found drugs, the contraband would be turned over to customs and the airline would get rewarded for finding drugs that customs had missed. Rewards amounted to mitigated former fines. The airline would be saving money and customs would be happy because more drugs would be confiscated. In theory, everyone would be thrilled.

"The General's got the contract. He wants me to run the show." Abe beamed.

"Congratulations." If Abe was going to offer me a job, I would have to politely decline. I swore that after working for the city of New York for twenty-two years I would never work steadily for one employer again. I didn't want a genuine job.

Abe looked around conspiratorially. "Well, we got this little problem."

In the General's rush to get the ball rolling he had never realized that in the state of New York one needs a license to conduct a security business. Neither Abe nor his uncle was eligible for a private investigator's license, which is what they were told they needed. The General didn't strike me as a very bright guy, for reasons I will explain later. I was beginning to wonder if the General was one of those military geniuses who thought invading Cuba would be a good idea. *Hey, this Bay of Pigs place seems like a good spot.*

Over dessert, Abe made the pitch. "We'll work under your PI license and we'll give you a cut, say a buck per man hour."

"How many man hours we talking about?"

He told me the name of the Caribbean airline we would be working for. "Maybe four hundred hours a week. Customs sees it's working, we get a few more airlines. We're talking maybe five, six carriers. Most are bigger than this one." He squinted. Multiplying must be tough for a business tycoon. "Your end will probably be somewhere around two thousand a week."

I made sure I wasn't liable financially for lawsuits, acts of God, or anything else that might arise before I agreed to get involved. Abe and I would run the show, the General was busy subverting a small government or something. The following week we rented an office (Abe signed the lease) and purchased a computer (Abe used his American Express card). He even bought lunch every day. It's nice to be appreciated.

Abe was to attend an important meeting with airline officials prior to the kickoff of business, which was in about three weeks. Since he didn't know shinola about the security business, I was coerced into going. Abe would be along to schmooz with the airline big shots. He was a good schmoozer. The morning of the meeting we met in our new office in Queens to discuss strategy. On the way out the door, Abe handed me a yarmulke.

"What am I supposed to do with this?" I asked.

"Put it on, you're supposed to be an Israeli." He grinned sheepishly. "I guess I forgot to tell you."

Abe, the idiot, had told the airline people that the entire security operation was being run by former Israeli commandos! I was one of them.

"Hey, look, that's the only way we could get the contract," Abe said. He grabbed me by the arm. "C'mon, we're gonna be late."

I shook myself loose. "Do you have *any* Israeli special ops people working for us?"

He nudged me toward the elevator. "Wags, you ever meet an Israeli that says he *wasn't* in the Mossad or a commando? What I did was go to Moishe's Movers and hire the guys off the boat that lug the pianos. They may be deadbeats, but I think they look like commandos." The meeting, surprisingly, went off without a hitch. A one-year contract was signed. We were in business.

I made my first and only demand the next day.

"I want to see the troops before they start work." Abe reluctantly agreed. About thirty young Israelis showed up at the office the following day.

The majority of them looked like they would be rejected from the Coast Guard. Most were in their early thirties, but it was plain to see that they weren't commando material. They were in poor shape. Too many brews between piano maneuvers. I had them dress-right-dress in a military formation in the hallway. I saw a lot of protruding guts.

"This won't do, Abe," I said. "The airline people will take one look at this crew and they're gonna know they've been scammed. What do the uniforms look like?" Abe brought out a sample: blue blazer with a company patch on the breast pocket, gray slacks, white shirt, and dark tie.

"You buy a lot of these?" I asked.

"I ordered forty sets."

"When?"

"Yesterday."

"Well, un-order them," I said. "I've got an idea." One week later we had the *new* uniforms: black fatigue shirts and pants, Corcoran jump boots, and the crowning touch—black berets. Each man would have a radio earpiece in his ear with a wire running into his shirt—attached to nothing. "*Now* they look like commandos." An old-time sergeant from The Job once told me that an ounce of image was worth a pound of performance. The sergeant was so incompetent he couldn't arrest a felon on Riker's Island, but he *looked* good. He always wore spit-shined shoes, and his shirt was ironed with military creases; he *appeared* to be the guy to go to when you needed help.

"You think this is better than my blazer look?" Abe was thinking like a civilian.

"Uniforms denote power, Abe. We're going to need some punch. The blazers make them look like insurance salesmen." The guys could move sofas, but I thought we needed them to look a little intimidating. "We're dealing with drugs here," I said. (When I was a cop on the Lower East Side of Manhattan I would sometimes stop a belligerent motorist. To take the wind out of his sails, I would force the motorist to donate his eyes after he died by signing his name in the appropriate spot on the back of his driver's license in lieu of a summons. Try doing *that* wearing a blazer.)

After we outfitted the troops, the bullshit paperwork began. Every man had to be fingerprinted, photographed, and trained. I had supervised a wide assortment of cops on The Job as a sergeant but the Israelis were the most undisciplined bunch of misfits I had ever run across. They had no sense of teamwork, constantly showed up late, and couldn't take direction. Amazingly, I whipped them into passable shape in the little time we had before we commenced our aircraft searches.

We hit a few minor snags during the first day of operation. I had assembled twelve men in a white van adjacent to the tarmac where our new client's flight was scheduled to land. After the plane touched down, I tried to use my airline access pass to get us through the gate onto the tarmac. The pass wouldn't work the gate so I had to drive to the adjoining gate, which belonged to Aer Lingus, the Irish airline.

Twelve fatigue-garbed "commandos" bounded from the van and rushed through Aer Lingus's area. People waiting to board a plane took one look at my guys and started screaming and hitting the floor, airline personnel included. I saw the panicked expressions on their faces and it said, loud and clear: IRA. These people thought the Irish Republican Army was staging a terrorist attack! It took a few minutes and changes of underwear before the Aer Lingus supervisors calmed down enough to let us through. We promised to get the correct passes the next time.

We approached our plane at a trot and were immediately surrounded by assault-rifle-toting Port Authority police. I had made sure that all the law-enforcement entities were aware of our presence at the airport, but apparently an Aer Lingus supervisor had dialed 911 and reported a terrorist assault on a plane. Another ninety minutes passed before the mess was straightened out. We boarded our first plane. We were operational.

Within our first week of business, my guys recovered ten kilos of marijuana from various aircraft. Keep in mind that this was *after* U.S. Customs had searched and cleared the *same planes*. I couldn't believe that customs was missing some of this stuff. Several planes had marijuana hidden in the pilot's compartment, placed there by mechanics in the Caribbean. Ground crews at JFK would sneak onto the plane at night and remove the contraband. Once this routine was discovered, you would think customs would be a little more conscientious.

My fledgling company made a name for itself very quickly. I was even proud of my misfits. Given the proper supervision, they turned out to be pretty crack troops. We began finding new hiding places on the planes. Our working relationship with customs was taking a beating because of this. They were pissed because we were making them look bad. There were even a few times when customs would find a load of drugs on a plane and we would board the same aircraft and find more. My guys weren't afraid to get dirty. These guys were furniture movers; they knew dirt. Customs agents wouldn't crawl around in the belly of a plane; my guys would.

I also discovered a scam of which customs was unaware. Some baggage handlers knew in advance which bags on certain planes contained drugs. Before the drug dogs got to sniff the luggage, the baggage handlers would off-load the bags that contained the drugs and store them in a separate area, only to return to them later and claim the booty. These handlers weren't apprised of the drug bags by secret code or clandestine radio message; the drug luggage had red ribbons tied around it. Real slick. It took an ex-cop to figure this out. After a while, a bag with a red ribbon attached to it announced: "I've got drugs inside me." Too many of these customs agents were from South Dakota and weren't that street smart.

But customs, to give them credit, came up with a surefire way to catch cocaine "mules." Flights from Colombia, via Avianca Airlines, would invariably have a few mules aboard. These individuals would swallow twenty or thirty tightly sealed condoms filled with cocaine and go straight to a safe house in New York to let nature take its course. Customs agents figured if someone downed thirty condoms they wouldn't be very hungry during the flight and wouldn't eat the meal offered by the airline. All customs would do was get the seat assignment of those people who refused meals and subject them to X rays when they passed through the customs declaration area. Agents are still nabbing mules this way.

The word was getting around that we knew what we were doing. This led to us picking up more airlines as clients. Money, needless to say, was rolling in. Of course, when things are going well, something always happens to screw them up. In this case it was Abe discovering that he didn't need me. While a license is needed to conduct a security business in New York, you don't necessarily need a *private investigator's* license. What is required is what's known as a watch-guard license, and anyone short of a convicted felon can secure one. My gravy train was about to come to an end. Since I had made no monetary investment in the business, I was just shown the door. Abe, to this day, is still at the airport confiscating drugs. We run into each other every so often and he always accuses me of knowing that he didn't need me from the outset. Who, me?

chapter nine

Manhattan's diamond district. West Forty-seventh Street between Fifth and Sixth avenues. More cash changes hands on that one street than anywhere else in the United States. Jewelers operate out of small storefronts and barricaded offices. Much of the business, however, is transacted right on the street, where a man's word is his bond and millions of dollars in diamonds can be seen, wrapped in handkerchiefs, passing from sellers to buyers. On this street, it's a man's world, businessmen consisting mostly of Hasidim and Third-World entrepreneurs.

The sidewalks are always packed during business hours. At night, the block is a tomb. Forty-seventh Street is one of the most security-conscious blocks in the world. If you walk down the street, be sure to smile. You're on someone's closed-circuit television monitor. At least one out of five "pedestrians" is an armed security agent or police officer. With all the scrutiny, you would think there would be little crime.

But reality rears its ugly head. The block is riddled with scam artists, armed robbers, pickpockets, and petty thieves. It's a security person's dream. Someone in my business could make a very good living on West Forty-seventh Street and never have to leave the block.

I had been trying for several years to work my way onto West Forty-seventh Street. Experience, honesty, and reliability are not enough to get yourself into that world. The security companies with a toehold guard their turf jealously and it's almost impossible to get work there unless you know someone. Over a period of years, I had made my phone calls, dropped names, and handed out business cards to operators of the large and small security companies that controlled the street. Finally, the phone rang on a chilly November day.

"Wags? It's Cooper Snowden. I'm overwhelmed."

"Why," I asked, "because you're talking to me?" Cooper Snowden's real name was Marvin Snowden-ski. He was a retired captain from The Job who had spent all his time with the NYPD hiding in firehouses studying for exams. The practice is known as "cooping," hence the nickname. Originally, Cooper had resented the nickname but after he'd retired, he'd thought it could work to his advantage. He had legally changed his last name to Snowden and passed himself off as the only New York City cop descended from British nobility. He'd taken elocution lessons to get rid of the Noo Yawk accent and had attacked the diamond district like it was Kaesong. Cooper was polished, that couldn't be denied. In ten years, he had most of the security contracts on the block sewn up.

"Very amusing, my friend," Cooper said. "No, it seems I'm overwhelmed with business. When last we spoke, you were looking for work. Is that still the case?"

"I'm always looking, Cooper." I'm overwhelmed with bills, I thought. He gave me the address of his new office. I was there within two hours.

I had to pass through two secretaries to get to Cooper. Both were young British women, or at least they spoke with English accents. Maybe they'd gone to Cooper's elocution teacher.

"Come in, Wags," Cooper said with an extravagant flourish of his arm. He was about my height but appeared shorter because he weighed at least three hundred pounds. I guess it's true what they say about firemen being good cooks. He was wearing an expensively cut charcoal gray three-piece suit that hid his bulk well.

I sank about six inches into an upholstered leather chair. I had to look up at Cooper—I think he'd planned it that way—who was seated behind a mammoth desk. His office overlooked the turmoil of Forty-seventh Street. We didn't waste words inquiring about each other's health or our respective family's well-being. Neither of us cared. Right down to business.

"Wags, have you ever made a . . . collection?" He said the word "collection" like he was speaking the Virgin Mary's name.

"When I had a paper route as a kid. Every Wednesday."

Cooper rolled his eyes. "Still the wiseguy, I see."

I smiled.

"On the street—Forty-seventh Street—most business is conducted with a handshake between retailers. Everybody trusts everybody. It's a policy that's made the block work for fifty years. Every so often, however, someone takes advantage of the system." He paused, making an elaborate ceremony out of lighting a big white pipe. Twenty years ago I remember him bumming Luckys from me. "It's mostly the new people, you understand, the Pakistanis, the Indians." He tossed a well-manicured hand. "Rubbish."

"I'm not a garbage collector, Cooper," I said, his effete attitude starting to piss me off.

"Oh, no, Wags," he said, "never would I group you with some of the strong-arm tactics that go on here. I need you for your diplomacy."

"Do I get diplomatic immunity?" I loved breaking his chops. He ignored the remark. I owed him one.

"What I'm referring to is bad debt between businessmen. Late payments, er . . . checks that may have crossed in the mail, that sort of thing." He explained that most of the work consisted of collecting money from individuals who bought jewelry on consignment and hadn't paid for it. "You must understand, Wags, after this money is collected, these men will go right back to doing business with each other. Some of them need a little—how shall I put it—push." Cooper explained to me that the faster I worked the more money I would make.

"I'll give you twenty percent of everything you recover, plus expenses. I would like you to work with someone—you can choose your own partner. This will obviate a 'he said, he said' scenario if there's ever a disagreement over, um . . . tactics." He smiled.

I had a brief moment of melancholy. Three years ago I'd been a sergeant on the NYPD. Now I was being asked to do money collections on the street. "What kind of debt are you talking about?"

Cooper stuck out a lower lip. "Oh, perhaps each debt in the fifty-thousand-dollar range."

I thought of my son's medical bills, and, I must admit, the lifestyle to which I was now becoming accustomed. When a normally moral person begins to disregard the code that has been a guideline all his life, it begins gradually. I've seen it happen to otherwise honest cops who begin their descent into corruption with one small, corrupt act. I had never gone down that crooked path on The Job, but I was coming to that fork in the road now. My only problem was that I didn't realize it.

"When do I start?"

"Immediately."

Most of the assignments had to do with consignment orders. A person on the street would buy a certain amount of jewelry and pay for it after it was sold. A good businessman would gradually increase the orders because he was a good salesman. What starts out as $10,000 on consignment can eventually, with ever increasing orders, turn into $50,000 in a short period of time. Cooper gave me a bunch of late-payment consignment orders and wished me well.

I needed a diplomat to work with, someone with a controlled temperament, well-spoken, and reliable. Well, one out of three isn't bad.

I went to a pay phone. "Hondo? Wags. You available for work?"

"Work, wha? Yeah, who?" As eloquent as ever. It was three in the afternoon and Hondo sounded like I woke him up.

"You know Cooper Snowden?"

"Cooper Snowden?" He was coming to life. "That's

an English car, ain't it? I think I had one of those. Yeah, a 1981 Cooper Snowden."

Hondo would do just fine.

The jobs went smoothly enough. The first week, no one gave us problems. Hondo and I would show up at a guy's office or store and our mere presence would guarantee that the check would be in the mail. We never even had to raise our voices. I was beginning to feel a little better about myself and rationalized that I was going to work in the morning like most other American husbands and fathers, performing mundane work and getting home in time for the six o'clock news.

Our first out-of-town job was in Chicago. While our first dozen or so assignments were in the $30,000 to $60,000 range, this one was a $120,000 bad debt. The deadbeat in Chicago had bought that much in gold chains and had failed to pay one cent on it. Before we left New York, I did a background on the debtor and found out he was into half a dozen shylocks for big money. The man had a gambling problem. Now he was about to have one more problem.

The man was an importer with an impressive operation. The day we went to his office he had at least ten people waiting to see him. We waited for over two hours like good soldiers, although Hondo did fifty push-ups on the carpet every half hour or so to keep from falling asleep.

The man greeted us cheerily until we told him we'd come for the money he owed Cooper's client.

"Tell that sonofabitch that he sold me inferior goods." He had a florid face and a shock of white hair that extended to his eyebrows. I figured him to be about forty-five—hard years—old.

"Then perhaps you'd like to return them," I said politely.

He came from around his desk. He stood about six feet four—I had to look up at him. Hondo casually turned sideways, expecting that all too uncomfortable kick in the balls. I figured I could sidestep him if I had to.

"You come here to strong-arm me?" our deadbeat said, his face getting even redder.

I said, politely, "Well, no, sir, I—"

"Do you know who I am? Do you know who I know?" He may have been big, but he was grossly out of shape and sported a bulbous drinker's nose and enough chins to hide a family of four. Whomever he counted among his friends, a plastic surgeon wasn't one of them.

Hondo appeared genuinely interested. "No, sir. Who do you know?" Our deadbeat rattled off a list of names preceded by titles—Congressman this, Councilman that.

"Politicians?" Hondo said and turned to me. "He knows politicians." Without waiting for a reply, Hondo whipped out a folding knife with a wicked curved serrated blade. Before the startled man could draw a breath, Hondo had grabbed his tie and sliced it off at the knot. He did it so quickly and *gently* that the man never even felt a tug. He was aware of what had happened when Hondo handed him a fistful of silk.

"Sir," I said, "could you come with me?" I put an arm around his shoulder and led him to his office window. I smelled his fear. I pointed fifteen floors down. He probably thought I was going to throw him out the window. "There's a coffee shop in that building. Are you familiar with it?" He nodded dumbly, unable to speak.

"My associate and I will be having lunch in there." I looked at my watch. "It's about that time. We'd like to see you there in one hour with cash. Understood?"

The deadbeat stammered understanding.

In the elevator I asked Hondo where he'd learned how to handle a knife so expertly.

"Videos."

Forty-five minutes later—while we were on dessert—a young woman delivered a cashier's check for $120,000 to our table.

I tried to treat the people we went after with respect. Most were just short of cash and had no intention of beating Cooper's clients out of money. They just needed a gentle reminder. Others, like our friend in Chicago, were gamblers or drug users who blew all their money on football games or cocaine. Those people we had to lean on. I didn't like myself for resorting to intimidation (we never hurt anyone), and while what we were doing was legal, it was a stretch from what I expected to be doing after twenty-two years of being a white knight. I was becoming more than a little greedy, but I promised myself that the collection jobs were just a bridge to other assignments that would be more professional in nature.

We'd been back from Chicago about a week when I got a surprising call from Cooper.

"Wags, do you remember a fellow named Walter Hartajian?"

Hartajian, I recalled, was one of the people we'd gone after for a $40,000 debt. He was a decent sort, just a little short of funds. He'd been in the jewelry business for fifteen years and enjoyed a good reputation. I knew he wasn't intentionally beating Cooper's client out of money, so we'd worked out a payment plan with him. Everybody was happy. All cases should end so well.

"Sure. Decent guy."

"Well, he was certainly impressed with you. He informs me you treated him like a gentleman. Now, it seems, he's got a rather serious problem and he thought of you. He's being shaken down by the mob." Cooper said Hartajian owed $15,000 to a jeweler on Forty-seventh Street who wasn't very patient and didn't feel like paying Cooper's "recovery" fee. Instead, the jeweler "sold" the debt to some wiseguys. The jeweler got all his money up front and the wiseguys doubled the debt to Hartajian. He now owed $30,000 to people he didn't know. "And if he doesn't come across within two weeks, there's going to be a point and a half per week interest."

One and a half percent interest a week on a $30,000 debt could add up to some serious money for a guy who didn't even have the original $15,000. "What does he need me for?"

"Bodyguard. It's your case; I choose not to get involved," Cooper said, which loosely translated is, "I don't want to end up as fish food."

I went to see Hartajian at his home in Bensonhurst, Brooklyn. I never expected him to be thrilled to see me. He was ecstatic.

"Oh, Mr. Wags, please come in." Hartajian had the hint of a Middle Eastern accent. He was wearing stylish baggy corduroy pants and a loose-fitting sweater. He led me by the arm into a sunken living room with white stucco walls and a roaring fire in a brass-gated fireplace. The furnishings were what wealthy people would call minimalist—two modular chairs and a sofa on a polished wood floor, with a low-slung coffee table dividing the room. An expensive entertainment system opposite the fireplace balanced the room.

Hartajian was about fifty, with a dark complexion, a slim build, dyed black hair, and wire-rimmed glasses. He had a drink in his hand when he answered the door. He smelled like vodka and appeared a little drunk. It was eleven o'clock in the morning. He offered me a drink. I declined.

I was seated in an uncomfortable chrome-and-leather chair when he told me about his cash-flow problem. Huge amounts were owed to him and he couldn't raise the money owed to the jeweler on short notice. When a six-foot late notice came to his door demanding double the original debt, he'd thought the man was making idle threats. Hartajian recalled the man dropping a lot of Italian names and saying he was connected to a Brooklyn "family."

"About a week later," he said, "we got a dead rat in the mail. My daughter opened the box." Tears came to his eyes. "She's only fifteen, Mr. Wags." The incident had occurred about three weeks before. Since then he had been getting threatening phone calls at the house and at his office in Manhattan. Hartajian's wife was so scared she hadn't left the house in three weeks. She was upstairs in their bedroom as we spoke. His daughter was staying with his sister, in Queens.

I had a feeling that the people making the threats were not connected mob people. Three of the calls were left on Hartajian's answering machine at home. Not very professional. If Hartajian was dealing with real mob guys, there would have been one or two personal visits, then something would have happened. They would at least have roughed him up or fire-bombed his car. Subtle messages. Dead men don't pay.

The bill was now up to $35,000, and climbing every day. The extortionists knew how to compound interest.

Hartajian wanted me to guard his family. Would I move into his house for a week? He was pressing his creditors to pony up some of the cash that was owed him. Banks, he said, were out of the question. He was mortgaged to his eyeballs. He had every intention of paying the wiseguys their money and assumed that within a week he would have enough cash to clear the debt.

There's no way to avoid crossing paths with orga-nized-crime figures in this business. I had met many "connected" men during the years since my retirement from The Job. While some in my business court their friendship, I do not. I treat them with respect but don't go out of my way to make friends. I like going to bed at night knowing I'm not being videotaped coming out of a restaurant with the FBI's current target of the month. I would break this rule very shortly and my life would turn around, but at that time my relationship with the mob was one of respectful distance.

I called an acquaintance who was an associate of a Brooklyn crime family. My Brooklyn wiseguy assured me that neither of the two Brooklyn families was shak-ing down Hartajian. In fact, my source was highly pissed off that someone would be using La Cosa Nos-tra's name in vain. He wanted to be kept apprised. Sure.

I signed on for $1,200 for the week. By that time, Hartajian said he would have the money to pay the extortionists. He wanted to get on with his life. I figured the shakedown artists for amateurs and didn't expect any trouble.

I accompanied my client to work every day. Hartajian's wife was still ensconced in their bedroom. I had yet to meet her. Without fail, when we arrived home there would be a threatening message left on the answering machine. I recognized at least three different voices over the first few days. They promised everything from disemboweling to deflowering Hartajian's daughter with a broom handle. The more they threatened, the more Hartajian drank. He was putting away at least a quart of vodka a day and reeled through his workday like he had rubber legs.

On the fifth day, he told me he was getting $40,000 that night, delivered in cash to the house from a guy in Manhattan who was coming through with the money he owed him. Hartajian was so happy his ordeal was about to end that he dragged his wife from her lair and they proceeded to party.

Mrs. Hartajian was about thirty-five and a real beauty. Dark, with jet black hair, she was a few inches taller than her husband and about ten pounds short of needing to lose weight. Big, but curvy in the right places. I would say, however, that she wasn't going to look good for very long. She made her husband seem like a teetotaler. The night she emerged from seclusion she put away a bottle of vodka in about three hours. She wasn't as good at holding the booze as hubby was. She began slurring immediately and had a habit of undoing a few buttons on her blouse when she got comfortable, which was after her third drink.

"She's got a drinking problem," Hartajian whispered to me when she made one of her frequent trips to the bathroom. No shit.

The money was delivered right after dinner. What we had to eat nightly, by the way, depended on the taste of the person who was sober enough to punch a phone number. I don't even think either of them knew where the kitchen was located. After five nights of Chinese food and pizza, I was having trouble fastening my pants.

Hartajian stayed home from work the next day, expecting to intercept the next phone call from the bad guys. It came at eight o'clock in the morning while I was in the shower. Hartajian was as white as a sheet when he told me about it.

"Now they want $60,000."

I had all in-coming calls taped. The man on the phone sounded like Don Corleone with a hangover. What follows is the transcribed conversation between my client and the Godfather.

Hartajian: Hello.
Godfather: Hartajian?
H: Yes.
G: You got the money?
H: Yes (barely audible).
G: Hah?
H: Yes!
G: You got the whole sixty large?
H: Sixty what?
G: Sixty thousand dollars, shithead!
H: But you said thirty-five!
G: That was before the family decided you was worth more (editor's note: give me a break!).

Anyway, you get the idea. While I was fiddling with my recorder, my client went up to the bedroom to tell his wife about the nasty turn of events. She did what any clear-thinking, level-headed victim might do. She called the FBI.

I've got nothing against the Federal Bureau of Investigation. Like any other law-enforcement agency, they are better at some things than they are at others. Solving New York City street crime is not their forte. In my experience as a New York City cop I've seen the bureau screw up an inordinate amount of cases, some that could have been handled successfully by a rookie detective. An odd phenomenon for sure, but I think directly related to the fact that many of the special agents working in New York City come from Jerkwater, Arkansas.

It must have been a slow crime day at 26 Federal Plaza, because within an hour the Hartajian home was swarming with feebies. It took a huddle of at least five agents to make the case for Hartajian's extortion problems to become federal problems. It was decided that the phoned threats constituted a federal crime. I must remind myself to watch my mouth the next time I yell at the cable company on the phone for not showing up between the hours of Monday and Wednesday. Hartajian wanted to keep me around after he saw what he was dealing with. I don't think the FBI was averse to my staying either. At least I knew where the Empire State Building was in case the cash was to be dropped there.

The two agents running the show were Fred Spahn and Hector Rodriguez. I figured Agent Rodriguez for a big-city kid but was disappointed to learn that he came from a small town in Mississippi and probably thought Taco Bell was a Mexican telephone company. He didn't speak Spanish and had a Southern accent you could cut with a knife.

They were nice enough guys but a bit lost. They strung the house with enough electronic recording equipment to make the Hartajian living room look like backstage at a Rolling Stones concert. Once set up, it took them at least three hours to figure out how the stuff worked. Spahn had to go to a local Radio Shack for backup batteries. But they were neat little soldiers. Every day they showed up in spiffy Brooks Brothers suits and brown wingtips. In the three days they were at the house, I took to calling them Spic and Spahn— behind their backs, of course.

The phone finally rang on the fourth day. Hartajian was instructed by a guy who sounded like Sheldon Leonard (am I dating myself?) to bring a suitcase filled with the sixty grand to a location in midtown Manhattan to be named in a later phone call. It was a short call and couldn't be traced.

All hell broke loose. Agents came from everywhere. Plan A, whatever the hell that was, was in effect. Hartajian would make the drop as ordered, only instead of a suitcase full of cash he would be traveling with a suitcase full of newspaper! Were those FBI guys sharp or what?

The entire operation would be monitored by twenty—I said twenty—FBI agents. In addition to the army of federal agents, a helicopter would be hovering overhead to capture the whole operation on tape, utilizing, of course, the latest whiz-bang, high-tech equipment. The landing at Utah Beach was planned with less care. What could go wrong?

That night Spic and Spahn stayed over and slept on the living room floor. I wasn't going to give up my comfortable foldout couch in the den, with the bar stuck up my ass, for anyone. I was exhausted and fell asleep around eleven o'clock. The last thing I remembered hearing was the agents deciding who was going to take the first watch. No one was going to take *them* by surprise.

I was awakened from a deep sleep by a cold hand on my shoulder. Instinctively, I grabbed for my gun before realizing that the hand belonged to Mrs. Hartajian. It was dark, for sure, but light enough for me to see that she was sitting on the end of the mattress holding a half-empty bottle of vodka and wearing a thin—*very thin*—negligee. She was quite drunk. They say vodka doesn't have an aroma, but she smelled like a cross between raw alcohol and leather, not all that unpleasant.

"Shhhh!" She made an attempt to put an index finger to her lips and jabbed herself in the eye. "I'm drunk."

I sat up. I was wearing my usual sleepwear—nothing—but I was covered by a blanket. "Coulda fooled me," I said, scooting as far as I could away from her while still maintaining what dignity I retained after being in my business for three years.

She leaned toward me. A breast dislodged from the negligee. I started to sweat. As groggy as I was, I didn't think a naked guy in bed right next to a woman with a breast exposed would look too good should someone walk in on us.

She giggled. "Oops!" She did a thing with her shoulder and her breast fell back into place. A neat move, I thought. "Hey, I'm scared for my husband tomorrow," she slurred. "You think it'll be okay?" She took a swig of vodka right from the bottle. I glanced toward the living room. Where the hell was the FBI? Whose turn was it to be up to watch for the enemy? I heard snoring. FBI, ever vigilant. Efram Zimbalist Jr. was going to hear from me.

"Look, Mrs. Hartaj—"

She smiled. Her eyes crossed and sparkled at the same time. "Call me Anna." She inched closer.

"Okay, Anna. I think it's best we all get some sleep. We've got a long day tomorrow, ya know, extortionists and all that." I was very nervous.

"Can't I stay here with you? I'm scared." She slipped a hand under the covers. She licked her lips. My God, didn't I see this in a porn movie once? Isn't the husband supposed to walk in now? Fuck it—I jumped off the couch and began to get dressed. If she was able to see past her nose, whatever I had she had seen before.

"Sorry, Mrs. Hartj—Anna, I gotta relieve the agent keeping watch. They work too hard." I zipped up and stumbled into the living room, colliding with an end table and knocking a phone to the floor. Spic and Spahn slept like they were dead. I collapsed on a couch and saw the shadowy figure of my new best friend tripping toward the stairs. She careened off every piece of equipment in her path. Finally she found the banister, which guided her back upstairs. The agents slept through it all.

The next morning the house was a proverbial beehive of activity. Two agents with headsets monitored the phone equipment, two were packing a hard-sided suitcase filled with folded newspaper and a wireless transmitter. Three more agents checked an assortment of long-distance eavesdropping gear, submachine guns—always popular in a gunfight in midtown Manhattan during a business day—and portable radios. Another agent was adjusting the straps on a bullet-proof vest. Spahn and Rodriguez were eating a brown-bag breakfast and discussing the merits of an Egg McMuffin vs. a ham and egg croissant.

Walter Hartajian came downstairs around eight o'clock. He was dressed in a wrinkled brown suit, white shirt, and brown tie. He was loaded. His eyes were glassy and he looked like he had been up all night drinking. Mrs. Hartajian was nowhere to be seen. Hartajian slurred a good morning, burped, and accepted an offer of an Egg McMuffin from Spahn. We waited for the phone to ring.

We were lulled into anticipatory silence. There was really nothing left to say. "The Plan" was in effect, equipment had been checked and double-checked. Hartajian was overflowing with booze-induced bravado, seething in a corner, nursing a drink. The missus came downstairs about nine o'clock, dressed in tight jeans, a red angora sweater, and four-inch-high black heels. Her hair was professionally tousled. Even Spic and Spahn stared at her. Those two guys hadn't glanced twice at her all the time they'd been in the house. I think they teach you in New Agents School to leave your dick at the office when conducting extortion cases involving lusty wives. She winked at me. I gave her a stony look. It wasn't easy.

The telephone rang at ten-thirty.

By that time Hartajian was so juiced he had to be helped to the phone. The agents had taken his bottle from him soon after he'd come downstairs but he left the room frequently. He probably had vodka stashed all over the house. Anna sipped a martini daintily throughout the morning. What a couple.

Hartajian stammered a hello. He was instructed to bring, at noon, the suitcase full of cash to the front of the Burger King on Seventh Avenue across from Madison Square Garden. He was to wait for instructions.

"And don't tell no cops!" yet another new voice warned. Our gangster had seen too many Humphrey Bogart movies.

An agent propped up Hartajian while another strapped him into a bulletproof vest. Still another outfitted him with a wireless transmitter. On top of that went an overcoat as big as Jackie Gleason's pajamas. All this on the warmest November day on record; it had to have been seventy-five degrees.

Spic and Spahn gave Hartajian instructions from both sides. Hartajian kept nodding like he knew what the hell was going on. I don't even think he knew what day it was.

On his way out the door, Hartajian's wife yelled, "Give the motherfuckers hell, Walter!" Sweetness and light. If he didn't get locked up for DWI, the operation might be successful.

Rodriguez, Spahn, and myself left by the back door. Hartajian had refused to cooperate unless I went as backup. A platoon of agents was already on its way to the drop location. I looked up, like Ray Liotta in *Good-Fellas* watching for the helicopter. I spotted it before we left the block.

Seventh Avenue and Thirty-third Street on a weekday afternoon during the lunch period can only be compared to Pamploma during the running of the bulls. Thousands of people rush like hell to get back to jobs they hate, all the while avoiding eye contact for fear of being beheaded by a homeless lunatic with a small hand ax hidden under a once worn London Fog raincoat donated by a flaming liberal who got a case of the guilts after watching Whoopi Goldberg rant on "Comic Relief." All this and twenty-odd federal agents armed to the teeth with automatic weapons searching for extortionists while eyeballing a drunk lugging around a suitcase full of old copies of *The Enquirer*.

A typical day in New York City.

Hartajian managed to get his car to a garage on Thirty-second Street without running any vehicles off the road or mowing anyone down. Special Agent Spahn parked next to a fire hydrant down the block from Burger King. We watched as Hartajian wove his way through the sea of pedestrians toward his meeting with destiny. He actually seemed drunker than when he'd left the house. It wouldn't have surprised me if he had a jug hidden in his car.

Hartajian was standing in front of the Burger King for maybe five minutes when a white guy about thirty approached him, said something, and took the suitcase. As soon as the man turned, Hartajian fainted. Right there in the middle of Seventh Avenue. Of course New Yorkers, being what they are, let Hartajian's head bounce off the concrete. No one stopped to help him. In New York, it's kindness if something like this happens to someone and pedestrians walk around rather than step directly on him.

The guy with the suitcase was wearing a gray suit and dark tie. He fit right into the business crowd. FBI agents came out of doorways, storefronts, buses, and the Burger King. The bad guy turned east on Thirty-third Street and entered an alley right next to the

143

Burger King. Spahn, Rodriguez, what seemed like the entire New York field office of the FBI, and myself pushed through the herd in an attempt to get into the alley. Other agents rushed to aid Hartajian.

The alley was a shortcut used by thousands of people. The guy with the suitcase handed off the suitcase to another man—we'll call him Bad Guy No. 2—who promptly entered a subway station.

Every agent was on his portable radio, talking at once. Mass confusion. No one, believe it or not, expected a second bad guy. Confusion reigned. No one knew who was supposed to follow whom. In the pandemonium, the original guy melted into the crowd and escaped.

A dozen FBI agents fell over each other getting down the subway stairs. They see Bad Guy No. 2 with the suitcase, his back toward them, calmly waiting for a train. The station had one of those turnstiles that is solid from floor to ceiling—it's a real barrier—and you must have a token to enter. There was no token clerk on duty.

I flew down the stairs in time to see twelve FBI agents cursing and screaming, yet unable to enter the platform. A train was whistling down the tracks. A young, good-looking woman with a skirt to mid thigh entered the gate and deposited a token. Two agents tried to jam themselves in the tiny space with her. One person can barely fit into one of those gates. She began screaming and elbowing the agent directly behind her in the testicles.

The train pulled into the station. The man with the suitcase waved without turning around and got on the train. Despite bloodcurdling screams from the agents—

one in contralto—the train slowly lumbered out of the station.

Everyone ran back upstairs. Spahn had the receiver, which was tracking the transmitter in the suitcase. It was beeping louder than a garbage truck in reverse. All hope wasn't lost. Rodriguez instructed the chopper, which had a duplicate receiver, to head downtown; the money was literally going south.

Traffic was a bitch. We were the lead car in a caravan of federal vehicles screaming downtown with lights and sirens wailing. In addition, we had the luxury of an agent from Alabama hanging out a window of our car yelling, "Get out the fucking way, ya'll!"

The transmitter signal went dead at the World Trade Center. The World Trade Center consists of two of the tallest buildings in the world, and the train our suitcase-carrying extortionist was on stopped directly under it. Fifty thousand people worked in those two buildings. It took three hours to find the suitcase, broken into of course, in a men's bathroom on the forty-ninth floor.

The FBI was so embarrassed that they'd screwed up the surveillance that they bowed out of active participation in the case. They told Hartajian that if the extortionists contacted him again to give them a call. Hartajian would sooner have called the Three Stooges.

A week later, one of the shakedown artists called again. He identified himself as "Tommy." He wasn't afraid of the FBI, he said (who could blame him?), and he wanted his money. Now the nut was up to $90,000. Hartajian called me. I hatched a plan.

Now the drop was to be made at a McDonald's in Connecticut, off the New England Thruway. The cash was to be left in a paper bag in a Dumpster adjacent to the McDonald's. I stuffed the bag with newspaper and a large piece of cardboard taken from a dry-cleaning package. On the cardboard I wrote down the phone number of a pay phone located about four miles from the drop sight.

I took Hondo, who came armed with three guns; I was the backup. We made the drop and went to the pay phone. Twenty minutes later it rang.

I picked it up and didn't wait for a response. "Dickhead," I said, "listen to what I'm gonna tell ya." I was doing my Joe Pesci imitation. "You're not dealing with the numbnuts FBI anymore. Hartajian came to me." I gave him the name of a made guy in Brooklyn who's a certifiable psycho. I knew these guys weren't connected to my friend in Brooklyn. I didn't hear a peep, just a lot of heavy breathing. "You guys ain't friends of ours. You ain't friends of nobody. I checked. Ain't shit goin' on I don't know about. My good friend Walter gets one more call from you, I'm gonna find you and pluck your fuckin' eyes out." I thought that was a nice touch. I banged down the phone with so much force I shattered the handset.

These guys were dumber than the FBI. Hartajian never heard from them again. I still get Christmas cards from his wife.

chapter ten

The closest most private investigators ever get to international intrigue is watching James Bond movies. Our business involves the mundane sometimes turned tragic or comical. My association with spies is limited to New York newspaper gossip columnists (something I'll discuss later).

After the Hartajian fiasco, I was relegated to my usual collections on Forty-seventh Street and a few fidelity cases. I was keeping out of trouble and paying my bills. Beau Dietl, my PI buddy from the Denmark case, someone whom I hadn't heard from in a while, paged me one day while things were slow and I was working out in the gym. He offered what he called a "routine" bodyguard assignment to guard an attorney whom I had heard of and his client. Both had received threats involving a federal case. I had less than an hour to get to the lawyer's office in Manhattan.

"I'm wearing jeans and a sweatshirt, Beau. I'm in the gym pumping iron. My gun's at home."

"You won't need a gun. Today's just a meeting. If you're wearing pants, you're overdressed. Just get down there."

Gus Periopolous, the attorney, had an office in downtown Manhattan. The address is a typical lower-Manhattan skyscraper housing an inordinate amount of attorneys. Gus's office was on the twenty-first floor, and unlike his brethren, his was a small suite with one secretary. A former federal prosecutor, these days he was defending mostly high-level drug dealers. His motto was, "Give me twenty-two grand and I'll give you a dismissal."

After I was announced, he came breezing out of his office and started pumping my hand. Periopolous was a bundle of nervous energy in a dark, three-piece, lawyer's uniform.

"Wags? Beau says all good things about you. Come inside." He practically pulled me into a small but expensively furnished office. He pointed to a leather chair. "Sit." I sat.

He immediately began leafing through pages in a manila folder, humming as he went along. He looked over the top of his reading glasses. "You ever hear of Jack Cervone?"

"I—" Before I could tell him that I had read the name in the paper, he interrupted me.

"Cervone's under indictment in the southern district for selling military supplies to the Iranians." He leaned back in his chair and adjusted his tie. He was a small, wiry man, wound tight, the type of guy who couldn't look you in the eye when he talked to you. He had a habit of pursing his lips between thoughts. He constantly rubbed his fingers together. He made me want a Valium just for talking to him. "He's been getting threats . . . hell, I've been getting them too."

"Threats from who?"

"Who the hell knows? Cervone's involved in everything." He lowered his voice. "Strictly off the record, of course."

"Of course. What's he *accused* of selling to the Iranians?"

"C-130s."

"C-130s? You mean military aircraft?" Periopolous nodded. He had said "C-130s" like he was describing stolen car radios. "This guy have a job?"

"He owns a gun shop in Brooklyn." How appropriate. "The point is, he's innocent." He raised his voice when he said "innocent" for the benefit of those who might be listening. "However, it doesn't look good for him in court. There's a witness for the prosecution who puts him at the scene with a bunch of ragheads and a lot of money."

"So why the threats?"

"My client knows where there's a pile of Iran-Contra money stashed. He's using it as a bargaining tool for a reduced charge and a cop-out. You know, maybe we plead him to attempted possession of a water balloon or something." He laughed at his own joke. "Some people want to shut him up before he opens up another can of worms. We've gotten a few phoned-in threats—testify and die—that sort of thing." I knew the Iran-Contra investigation had officially ended a few years before. Could Cervone be the catalyst that reopened the case? "We need you around for the threats and we need you to go with us to Chicago, where the money's stashed. We get the money, come back, turn it over to the federal prosecutor. A good-faith gesture."

"How much we talking about?" I asked.

"Cervone says two million dollars or thereabouts. There's also supposed to be some incriminating paperwork in with the cash, exactly what we won't know till we pick it up."

Something didn't make sense. "So he hands over the cash, what's he got left to bargain with?"

Periopolous got up and jammed the papers back into the folder. He smiled. "My client tells me he knows where another five million is buried." He came from behind his desk. "C'mon, let's go meet Cervone."

Jack Cervone was about fifty and made Periopolous look like Perry Como. We were in a coffee shop in downtown Brooklyn that was jammed with customers. Cervone sat with his back against a wall, eyes bouncing from the front door to the kitchen, eyeing everyone who walked in no matter what their age or physical condition. Cervone was scared witless and it showed. He was wearing black slacks, a black silk shirt, and a gray leather sports jacket. His gold Rolex spoke well for the current condition of the *pistola* business.

"Who's this guy?" he said, pointing to me. I slid in the booth, opposite him. Periopolous made the introductions but Cervone eyed me like I was about to stab him in the heart. We ordered lunch. The lawyer tried to make small talk but Cervone didn't have much to say. He kept one eye on me, one eye on the front door, and one eye on the help coming in and out of the kitchen. Try it sometime and see if that doesn't get you agitated.

"Wags," Periopolous said after biting into a tuna sandwich on toast, "Jack, you, and I are going to Chicago. When we—"

Cervone leaned forward. "I ain't goin' no fuckin' where." He had jet black hair culminating in a wicked-looking widow's peak. He looked a little like Jack Nicholson on a bad-dye day. He was pushing the envelope a little with the show of bravado. Cervone struck me as the type of guy who, if he was home alone, closed the door to the bathroom when he peed.

Periopolous was momentarily speechless. I bet that hadn't happened too many times in his lifetime. "What, are you crazy? We gotta get the money. The case goes to court tomorrow."

"Oh, yeah?" Cervone said. "Well, you go get the goddamn money, I'll tell you where it is. People die in plane crashes, you know what I'm sayin'? The fuckin' things have a habit of blowin' up." Cervone was paranoid. Sweat was trickling from his forehead. "And another thing: Why do I have to go to court? Can't I stay in the hotel room or somethin'?"

"You're the goddamn defendant, for Christ's sake!" A few customers looked in the direction of the outburst. Periopolous lowered his voice. "You know I'm working on a few things for you." Periopolous glanced quickly at me. I think things were going on I wasn't supposed to know about.

They argued for ten minutes. Cervone was certain he was going to get whacked somewhere between the hotel where he was staying and the courthouse downtown. Traveling to Chicago was out of the question because he was convinced someone would take the plane out with a surface-to-air missile. Finally, Periopolous threw up his hands in defeat. He turned to me.

"You have someone can baby-sit my client here?"

"Hey," Cervone exclaimed, "no one—"

Periopolous whirled on his client. "Shut the fuck up! I'm trying to save your sorry ass from thirty years in prison." I wondered if Perry Mason would ever admonish his client like that. Cervone lowered his eyes and sat back in his seat. He sighed.

"Now," the attorney said, "as I was saying—"

"Yeah, I've got someone who could watch him. Reliable guy." Hondo, if I could find him, wouldn't take Cervone's crap.

"Good. Get him on the horn. I'm calling the airline for flight times. You and I are going to Chicago."

"Now?" I said. "I'm not armed. I've got twenty dollars in my pocket. Give me a few—"

"We haven't got a few anything." He looked at his watch. "I'm not concerned about our safety today. Who the hell knows we're here? Who knows we're going to Chicago? It's tomorrow I'm worried about. To and from court. Jack's got a point."

I was getting a little paranoid myself. "No one knows we're going to Chicago today? You make plane reservations?"

"What, do you think I'm stupid? We'll go to La Guardia right now, get the tickets at the gate."

I paged Hondo. He got back to me in ten minutes.

"You rang?"

"If you're not busy, I need you to baby-sit a lawyer's client." I told him where I was and what the job entailed. "All you gotta do is make sure he stays put in the hotel. I'll tell you where he's staying when you get down here." We settled on his daily fee.

"I'll be there in less than an hour."

By the time Hondo arrived, we had gone through two pots of coffee. The lunch crowd had dissipated, which made Cervone even more paranoid. Now he was sure that a politically correct hit man would come in and spray the joint with automatic weapons' fire and not fear hitting innocent civilians.

Hondo was dressed in an olive-colored Armani suit and matching overcoat. His shoes shone like a thousand suns. He was the only guy I ever knew who spit-shined his Guccis. Once a Ranger, always a Ranger. I introduced Hondo to Cervone and Periopolous. Hondo nodded but didn't shake the offered hands. In addition to all his other quirks, Hondo was paranoid about germs. Hondo and Cervone had what could be termed an adversarial relationship right from the start.

"This fucking guy ain't watching me," Cervone said. "I don't like his attitude." Hondo replied by hitting Cervone on the side of the head with an empty coffeepot. Not a vicious blow, just something to get his attention. It happened so fast that the pot was back on the table before the few remaining customers in the coffee shop could react.

"What the fuck!" Cervone's eyes were crossed. He rubbed the side of his head. Periopolous didn't say boo.

"You're lucky, he must have left his knife at home," I said. I turned to Hondo, who was breathing ever so slightly more deeply. He was pissed but under control. For the next ten minutes, Hondo stared at Cervone while Periopolous and I went over the travel plans. Cervone avoided Hondo's riveting glare. He was now under control, which was what Hondo had wanted to begin with.

It was decided that Hondo would escort Cervone back to the Sherry Netherland Hotel while the lawyer and I took a taxi to the airport. I spoke to Hondo alone before we went our separate ways.

"He may boogie on you, Hondo. He's scared to death of going to court tomorrow, thinks someone is going to whack him."

"Yeah, me."

"Do me a favor, shoot the sonofabitch *after* the trial. Which reminds me, you got an extra gun?"

Hondo looked furtively around the foyer of the coffee shop. "What do you need, a nine? Maybe something smaller?" He opened his jacket to reveal a Glock nine millimeter in a belt holster on his waist. "I also have one of these." He raised a pant leg to reveal a tiny automatic. "Take your pick."

I pocketed the little .32. Even though the gun wasn't on my license, I would rather explain to a grand jury how it saved my life than be caught short without it. Periopolous and I waited for Hondo and his charge to find a cab and drive toward Manhattan. We got into our own taxi and started for the Brooklyn-Queens Expressway and La Guardia Airport.

"We have to make one stop before we get to the airport," Periopolous told me and gave the cabbie directions to the Pan Am Hotel on Queens Boulevard.

We were met in front of the hotel by a man about fifty years old wearing a fatigue jacket and a raggedy pair of jeans. He was unshaven and looked like he had slept in his clothes.

"Watch our backs, Wags," Periopolous said. "I need

to talk to this guy for a few minutes." He didn't make introductions. I told the cabbie to wait.

While they talked in front of the hotel, I scanned the street. The hotel is located on an eight-lane road that is heavily traveled. Anyone in the thousands of cars that passed could have taken a shot at us. Periopolous seemed unconcerned. The man he was talking to made sure that the lawyer's body was between him and the passing traffic.

I wanted to stay close enough to them to warn them of potential danger but at the same time I didn't want to be privy to their conversation. What I didn't know couldn't get me indicted. I caught snippets, however.

". . . Fifty thousand dollars . . ."

". . . Mossad . . ."

". . . CIA . . . renegade agents. . . ."

What the hell had I gotten myself involved in? All of a sudden the minuscule .32 auto I was packing seemed woefully inadequate. After five minutes of intrigue, we got back in the cab and started on the ten-minute ride to the airport.

"Everything okay?" I asked, wanting reassurance.

"Everything's fine, Wags. You know who that guy was?" He mentioned a name I have since forgotten. "Former big wheel in the CIA."

"He looks like a shopping-bag man."

Periopolous smirked. "Maybe that's because he's living in a sleeping bag in Central Park. He's on the lam from the FBI because of the Iran-Contra investigation. He also thinks some of his former colleagues are out to shut him up."

"He's important to Cervone's case?"

Periopolous put a finger to his lips and removed a

slip of paper from his pocket. There was a Chicago address written on it. "This is where we're going."

I nodded, assuming that's where the money was, but didn't say as much, not wanting to share the information with a Pakistani cabdriver.

We were waiting in line in La Guardia's main terminal to get our tickets when Periopolous turned to me and said, "You know, Wags, if anything happens to you, your family will be taken care of." He smiled benevolently.

How comforting. "That's nice. What's my name?"

This would be the second time in his life he was rendered speechless. He stared at me dumbly. "Huh?" I repeated the question.

"Well, uh . . ." He was his usual nervous self, only now he was also tongue-tied. Terminal for a lawyer.

"What are you going to do, send a check to Mrs. Wags? You don't even know my name, how the hell are you going to take care of my family?" I put my arm around him. "Tell you what, someone tries to take me out, I'll shoot you so they won't take you prisoner."

He didn't know whether I was kidding or not. I'm sure he doesn't to this day. Neither do I. He smiled apprehensively. "Very funny."

Periopolous paid for our tickets with cash. I deposited my gun in a locker. I had no choice unless I wanted to share a cell with Cervone. If someone was sharp enough to track us to Chicago, I'd stand still so he could get a good shot.

The Windy City was a bust. We went to the supplied address. It turned out to be a Kentucky Fried Chicken store. Periopolous was upset. "Maybe we have to wait for someone." We waited three hours. I was getting impatient.

"Want some chicken?" I asked, sarcasm evident. He got the message. We flew back to New York.

When we got to La Guardia, a lightbulb went off in my head. I raced to a phone. Hondo answered on the first ring.

"Yeah?"

"Hondo, Wags . . . everything okay? What's Cervone doing?"

A moment's silence. "Watching TV. Why?"

"He make any phone calls?"

"Yeah, one. Practically had his head buried under a pillow, couldn't make out who he called."

"Don't let him out of your sight. We'll be there in about an hour."

Periopolous wanted to know what was going on. "Who set the meeting up with the CIA guy?" I asked.

"Cervone. Why?"

"Because, Counselor, he wanted you out of town. He's gonna cut and run. I doubt there's any money, at least not two million." There was a line of people waiting for taxis. We pushed our way to the head of it. No one stopped us. Welcome to New York, where everyone thinks *everyone else* is psycho.

Periopolous looked perplexed. "I don't get it." We were in a cab heading toward the Triborough Bridge.

"Cervone's scared to death. He's not about to stand trial. He gets you out of town so you won't take any heat and he splits."

"So I won't take any heat?" Periopolous was angry. "I've got a half-assed deal with the federal prosecutor! He's expecting me to walk into court tomorrow with two million bucks! Jesus Christ! Not only won't I show up with any money, but maybe I won't have my client there either."

"Hondo's watching him," I said reassuringly. "Cervone's not going anywhere."

Periopolous seethed while I guided the non-English-speaking cabbie across side streets to avoid traffic. We pulled up in front of the Sherry Netherland Hotel in record time.

The lawyer was behind me as I approached the revolving door that led to the lobby. As I started to walk through, Cervone came flying out of the hotel like his ass was on fire. He was struggling into his leather jacket. When he saw me, he made an abrupt one-eighty and took off down Fifth Avenue. Periopolous just stood there, mouth agape.

Hondo came out of the hotel a second later like he'd been shot out of a cannon. He was struggling to fasten the belt on his pants. "Sonofabitch!" he hollered when he saw me, "the motherfucker ran when I was in the john!" We both took off after him.

Cervone turned east on Fifty-ninth Street. He was no match for Hondo, who pounced on him before he had run a block. I was there to help in seconds. Hondo had Cervone in a headlock and was trying to walk up crowded Fifth Avenue like he was out for a stroll with a mannequin. I walked interference in front of them. A few people glanced our way but quickly averted their gaze when they saw the crazed look in Hondo's eyes. Cervone was struggling for breath; Hondo knew enough to relax his grip when Cervone was about to pass out, only to tighten it again when Cervone got vocal.

Cervone promised to be a good boy while we were waiting for the elevator. We rode to the thirtieth floor in silence. When we got to the room, Periopolous lit into his client. The harangue lasted ten minutes. Cervone admitted to the ploy. He said he knew as much about Iran-Contra as Ronald Reagan. I detected a smile. He used the possibility of turning over the Iran-Contra money to buy time to make escape plans. He was scared for himself and his family. He didn't want to go to jail. I hate to admit it, but I felt sorry for the guy.

Periopolous took me into the bathroom. "Look, Wags, I appreciate everything you've done. I've gotta get myself out of a helluva fix and I'd rather not have you around while I do it. Understand?"

"Perfectly."

We left, promising to be at the hotel the next morning at seven. Hondo acted like a dejected schoolkid.

"Jimmy, I'm sorry about that asshole getting loose. You don't have to pay me. This one's on me."

It took me the entire ride back to Staten Island to finally convince Hondo that we all made mistakes. He took his pay.

The next morning we were back at the Sherry Netherland armed to the teeth. Even though the Iran-Contra story was so much crap, Cervone might still be a threat to some people involved in the C-130 case.

Cervone seemed more relaxed. But Periopolous was even more manic than the day before. I suggested we take a subway to court. Ambushing a cab caught in the morning rush was too easy.

Courthouses always impress me. That friend of mine I mentioned earlier who was a paratrooper once told me he still gets goosebumps when he hears a military march even though he's been out of the army for thirty years. I feel the same way about entering a courtroom. No matter how cynical most cops get, the effect that symbol of the justice system has on us is profound. We still believe in the system. I didn't know it that day, but the next time I would enter a courthouse would be as a defendant.

The courtroom was still locked when we got upstairs. We were early and had about an hour to kill. For security reasons, I had everyone stay in the hallway. Periopolous got more agitated as time passed. He paced the entire length of the hallway several times, ringing his hands so often I thought he would twist them off at the wrist. I knew him to have spent most of his career in a courtroom. Why the hell was he so nervous now? I asked him about it.

"I've got a do-or-die plan. I called the prosecutor at home last night and came clean. He's pissed about Cervone's bullshit story. I could be looking at a complaint against me with the bar."

"Unless you win the case?" I offered.

He smiled weakly. "Unless I win the case." He looked at his watch for the fiftieth time. Hondo's eyes lit up.

"Hey, Counselor, nice watch." Hondo may lack grace but he knew his accessories.

Periopolous seemed distracted. "Huh? This watch. You like it?"

Hondo blinked. "Yeah, sure. It's nice."

Periopolous took it off his wrist. "Here you go, it's yours." He tossed it to a surprised Hondo.

"Hey, man, I can't take this," Hondo said, trying to force it back on the lawyer. Periopolous wouldn't hear of it. They argued for a few minutes.

Finally, I said, "Give it to me, I'll take it." Hondo looked at me, then to the lawyer.

Periopolous shrugged. "Give him the goddamn thing." Hondo handed it to me. It was a Raymond Weil, probably worth around a thousand dollars. I offered my Wittnauer in exchange. Periopolous refused. I still have the watch.

The only reason I bring up this vignette is that the whole scenario was a microcosm for what I had become. Since I had gotten into the security business, *things* meant everything to me. Previously, material objects, money included, had never ruled my life. I didn't realize it at the time, but my new moral standards would soon land me in jail.

The prosecutor called his first witness, a well-dressed man of about forty who was supposed to place Cervone at the scene of the C-130 deal. The prosecutor's own witness proved to be a dud. Under a skillful cross-examination by Periopolous, the witness vacillated and admitted he wasn't *absolutely* certain that Cervone was the person who had made the illegal deal. It was, after all, he said, five years ago.

The federal prosecutor called a recess. He and Periopolous were called into the judge's chambers. Cervone waited with me for about fifteen minutes before he was also summoned into chambers. If he seemed unusually tranquil before the meeting, he was almost comatose when he came out.

All parties assembled in front of the judge. The prosecutor was dropping all the charges except the most minor and was allowing Cervone to plead to a low-level felony! Cervone accepted the plea bargain and was sentenced to one year in jail, minus time served.

He would be out in five months. He had thirty days to surrender.

Periopolous and Cervone walked out of court arm in arm.

"Meet me at San Domenico for dinner, say around eight o'clock," Periopolous said to me as he breezed by. "Bring Hondo. We're gonna have a celebration dinner."

I showed up a half hour early at the fancy Italian joint on Central Park South. I generally show up early for every meeting. I hate surprises. Hondo, dressed like he owned the place, was right behind me.

At eight-fifteen Periopolous strolled in with Cervone and a guest: *the prosecution's star witness*.

This was the person whose sudden lapse of memory had caused the government to offer Cervone the plea bargain. Now he was having dinner with the defendant! I decided I wasn't that hungry. Hondo was already out the door. I begged off, complaining of a vicious headache. The victors didn't care, they were in a partying mood.

I decided to take a stroll through Central Park and have a cigarette before I went home. I laughed to myself, thinking that I might meet up with that rogue CIA agent we'd met in Queens. It was a brisk autumn night and one of the few evenings I can recall when stars were visible. The park is a beautiful oasis in a desert of grime, often given a bad rap as crime-ridden at night. Actually, it's one of the safest places in the city, patrolled by enough cops to secure the black hole of Calcutta.

That night I felt dirty. I suddenly realized who'd gotten that $50,000 I'd heard mentioned during the lawyer's meeting with the ex-CIA big shot. But I rationalized my way to a clear conscience. I had had nothing to do with any unsavory deals that might have been made and I certainly wasn't privy to any concrete proof regarding anything illegal that might have taken place.

My ability to justify my actions would soon have disastrous results.

chapter eleven

Over the years, whenever I met rookie police officers, I would ask why they had joined the NYPD. I would mostly get the same answer: "Because I wanted to help people." Every now and then I'd find a candid young cop who would tell me: "Because I wanted to lock up bad guys and get the mutts off the street." Invariably, the cop who was more aggressive and straightforward would be the better police officer. Most of the I-want-to-help-people variety wound up helping people from a desk job. It might be a flawed survey, but I found the results to be accurate. My buddy who served in an airborne unit in the army said it best when he was asked why he had volunteered for Vietnam: "Because I want to blow shit up." This statement comes from a good family man who has a master's degree and runs a successful business. He was, might I add, a helluva soldier.

Good cops, like good soldiers, crave excitement. I knew I was rarely helping anyone when I was on the street. I was either locking someone up, summonsing them, or notifying a parent that their kid had just OD'd. It might be a cynical attitude, but honesty compels me to say I was in police work for the thrill of it. The people I helped along the way were invariably aided by me because I had just taken a rapist off the street who might have assaulted them the next day.

This "thrill-of-the-kill" attitude prevails in any good cop. I have seen even the most corrupt officers on The Job risk their lives rushing to be the first on the scene at gun runs to aid their fellow officers. Corruption is a form of thrill, thankfully, that most cops avoid, but the quest for a "kick"—not the money involved—drives some cops over the edge.

The thrill of the kill costs some cops their lives. Ignoring a slightly opened doorway in a darkened hallway because you're in a hurry to get the man with the gun in the next apartment, taking your eyes off people in the backseat of a car momentarily to give one or all of them an edge to go for a weapon can give a cop a rush. After a while it's the way you do your job and you don't give it a second thought. It's cheaper than bungee jumping and you don't have to look for a bridge. Bravado, however, can lead to carelessness and an inspector's funeral.

My love of taking chances came with me when I left The Job. The Istanbul and Denmark assignments made that evident. But I was almost unaware of some of the chances I was taking and was becoming convinced—subconsciously—that I was indestructible. It also seemed that the more money I made, the more I wanted. The crusade for more dollars was actually a crusade for more thrills. I realize that now, but then I was oblivious to my motives.

I should have been more than content. My son's illness had disappeared. All his hospital bills had been paid. My relationship with my wife and kids had never been better. Business was booming. But still I wanted more. Not the money, the next job that would provide a kick. I had finally reached a point in my life where the next "big job" wasn't enough. The bubble had to burst. Trouble was waiting with a sledgehammer to knock on my door. When it came, it arrived in the form of sixty topless women. The downward spiral was about to begin and I was too self-absorbed to realize it.

If New York City is the financial capital of the world, it is going for statehood where the sex industry is concerned. During the initial 1980s AIDS scare, the sex business in the city all but petered out (pun intended). The gay community bore the brunt of AIDS paranoia. Bars and clubs that catered to a gay clientele were closed down if "unsafe sexual practices" were committed. Heterosexual sex clubs, which kept lower profiles, were harassed sporadically but not generally subjected to media attention. Our mayor back then championed the impossible cause of changing people's sexual behavior while ignoring an ever increasing crime problem. But that's another book.

High-end topless clubs became popular around this time. Topless *bars* have been around forever; what I'm talking about here are major clubs where investors spent millions of dollars turning former discos into nirvanas of flesh. The predominant clubs, like Stringfellows and Scores, were the first kids on the block. They provided the affluent businessman with the opportunity to ogle beautiful women close up,

spend mountains of money, and not have to worry
about bringing AIDS home to the missus. As an extra
added bonus, they could charge it all to their businesses. Men that frequent these clubs are aware of the
strictly enforced hands-off policy but harbor a fantasy
that a drop-dead gorgeous dancer will disregard the
rules and go home with *them*. And, of course, these
women could *never* be diseased, they're too goddamn
good-looking! These are the same types of guys who
go to the automobile show every year at the Javits
Center expecting to score with models hawking next
year's Buicks.

As in any other business where enormous amounts
of money are made, there's a certain amount of trouble
endemic to topless clubs. The clubs need a number of
investors to get off the ground—moneymen. After millions of dollars are lined up, what you've got is a
bunch of well-heeled businessmen who want to open a
topless club and haven't the slightest idea how to do it.
This is where the promoters get involved.

The promoters do everything from getting the army
of topless dancers to getting the place painted. A good
promoter has a "stable," or "book," of five thousand
women ready to take their clothes off. The women answer to the promoters, not the owners. Promoters are
generally under contract for a year. For their efforts
they get a piece of the action, a percentage of the net.
Often, the more successful the promoter, the more
problems he lets himself in for. What happens is that
the club becomes a money machine because of the
savvy of the promoter. Everyone involved is making
money. This should lead to harmony but it often kick-
starts the greed engine. The owners figure after a while
that they don't need the promoter—hell, they've been

in business for three months, they know everything there is to know. Why not muscle out the promoter— the person who made it all possible—and keep *all* the profits? Situations like these usually work themselves out, often with the promoter renegotiating his contract for a smaller percentage just to keep the peace and keep the bucks rolling in. When both parties get testy, the troops have to be called in. Call me George Patton.

The majority partner for a new club on Manhattan's east side had me come to his office for a chat. I'll call the club Topsey's because it's still in operation and is involved in court battles with everyone from the liquor salesmen to the janitor. The owner's name was Stuart and he was pissed.

"I'm throwing thousands of dollars away every day on a promoter who did his job before we opened up and hasn't stepped a foot in here since." We were sitting in a nicely furnished office above the club on a cold January night. It was close to midnight but a skeleton office staff was on hand shuffling paper and looking busy. Stuart was under thirty, expensively dressed in a dark business suit and paisley tie. His tan looked natural and his accent said Florida. I found out later that he had managed a string of topless clubs in South Florida called Pure Platinum and Solid Gold before going out on his own. Topsey's was his first venture into ownership.

"I thought that's what promoters do—set the place up and leave," I said.

Stuart lit a Cuban stinker. "Yeah, but they get points till the contract's up. It's bullshit. I can get them out if they break the contract. That's why you're here. I need you to watch the girls—tell me what they're doing."

"Like what?"

He came around his desk and walked to a poster-size mirror on the opposite wall. He pointed over his shoulder. "Shut the light over there, will ya?"

I hit the switch. When the room went dark, the two-way mirror revealed the club one floor below us. "I've got sixty broads running around half naked at any given time. If any one of them does drugs on the premises, propositions a customer, or causes a fight, I could bounce the promoter out on his ass. It's on paper."

The club was crowded. At least two hundred men mingled with bare-breasted women. Some women were dancing on elevated stages, others were gyrating privately for individual customers. Twinkling lights made me think of a steeplechase with tits. Four nearly naked bartenders served drinks nonstop. We were in a soundproof office but the mirror vibrated with the beat of the music. Every customer wore either a suit or a jacket. Pinky rings glistened. Very civilized.

Stuart had found me through his attorney; I had done bodyguard work for him in the past. My job in the club would ostensibly be .as head of security. Bouncers were posted at the entrance to keep out drunks and to respond to disputes inside the club before they got out of hand. My cover would have me as their boss. I would draw a salary for that position plus my daily rate for spying on the dancers. If enough violations were documented, the promoter—whose responsibility it was to keep the women straight—could be removed. The entire mess was in court. My observations would be crucial for Stuart's case. I dusted off my tux and started the next night.

Topsey's didn't open until six o'clock. I got there at five and Stuart introduced me around. There were three bouncers on the door. They all looked like refrigerators. Two were ex-cops, one was still on The Job. They were congenial enough but I got the impression that they didn't like the idea of supervision. The inside help was more friendly. The female bartenders were stunning and topless. Stuart took me to a cavernous dressing room where at least forty dancers were dressing—or undressing. Every one of them was a beauty. He clapped his hands a few times and the buzz stopped. I was the center of attention, something I never figured would occur in a topless club. Trying to look the ladies in the face would be difficult.

"Ladies, this is Jimmy Wagner—you can call him Wags." Everyone cooed a hello. I was a little embarrassed. "He's your protector, your savior," Stuart said. "Anyone gives you a hard time, see Wags." He poked me in the side. "You can trust him." I knew these women were in a tough business and I wasn't expecting to be dealing with Virgin Marys, but I already felt a little guilty about having to spy on them; however, between the salary and my daily rate I would be pulling in three grand a week. I'd learn to live with myself.

I was introduced to the "house mom." The position was held by a former topless dancer who was a little bit long in the tooth to be dancing. It was the house mom's job to cater to the dancers' whims. If you rip something, see the house mom. Got that embarrassing run in the stockings you'll be peeling off? See the house mom. You get the idea. She was called "Droopy" by the bouncers, a name that referred to what might have been a prerequisite for the job. Her real name was Helen.

It took me three nights to get a feel for the place. The

club was one large room divided by a large black-enameled bar. To the right of the bar were several small stages and an elevated dining area protected by interlocking brass rails. The food, surprisingly, was quite good. I ate whatever I wanted. My arteries began to rebel from too much filet mignon. On the other side of the bar was a huge stage fed by a runway. Every two hours the dancers would assemble and parade down the runway. Each lady would be announced as she made her entrance. The customers would learn her name and where she hailed from.

The women made big money. There wasn't much of a turnover because a dancer could make three thousand dollars a night. Who would want to leave? Every Monday afternoon, however, there was an audition. Girls would show up from all over the world for a shot at a job. They danced to music they'd brought and were given a nod or shown the door. Dancers paid the house $75 a night for the privilege of working in Topsey's. They made money hustling private dances and tips.

Here's how it worked:

Topsey's sold what they called "funny money." These were house chits that looked like dollar bills. There was a 20 percent markup on this funny money. A customer purchased $1,000 in funny money and paid $1,200 for it. When the girls cashed in at the end of the night, they were charged an additional 10 percent. A double whammy. Corporate credit cards were the payment of choice. The credit card statement at the end of the month would indicate a purchase from "Global Food & Beverage." Wives perusing hubby's spending habits would think their spouses were having dinner with the United Nations secretary general. The IRS could have had a field day in the place.

Customers paid the girls with the house script. Everybody was happy. Personal, up-close dances by a nubile, bare-breasted young thing cost twenty dollars. A massage cost the same. Both were done to music, each song exactly the same length (short) so as not to spend too much time dancing or rubbing some guy's back to "A Bridge over Troubled Water." A massage would consist of a girl loosening a customer's tie and gently rubbing his neck and shoulders. A personal dance would be one-on-one with a customer. The customer would sit (or stand) while the dancer did her thing. No touching allowed.

The women were very aggressive when it came to pushing customers for massages or dances. A guy wouldn't be in the club two minutes before he'd be approached and hit on for twenty bucks. The house split the money with the girls. This could add up. Some customers had their own "steady" girls. Often a smitten customer would spend upward of seven hundred dollars for a particular girl's "favors" over a period of a few hours. That's enough massages to rub the skin off an armadillo. And he would never lay a hand on her. In a way, I guess he was getting screwed anyway. The girls also did well for dancing on stage. Twenties and fifties would be jammed into their minuscule dental-floss G-strings.

Drinks were $7.50 a pop, including spring water. Top-shelf stuff cost more. A magician roamed the floor making cards disappear. The house made money disappear. David Copperfield would be proud.

By the end of the third night, I realized that there was a lot more cash to be made than what I was drawing in salary and billing. Chet, the off-duty cop, took me aside and stuffed a wad of bills in my pocket. "Door tax," he said and went back outside. He later told me that the twenty dollars to get in the door was often boosted to double if someone wanted to buck the line to get in, and there was always a line. Limo drivers paid the bouncers to steer customers to them. The bouncers take the split at the end of the night. I got 10 percent for being the boss, or about $150 a night.

Then there were the customers who wanted to be recognized. If I smiled and called a customer by his name, it was good for at least a twenty. One steady big spender always sought me out when he came in and handed me a fifty. I'd have to make small talk for thirty seconds, just long enough for the girls to see him talking to me. This made him feel like a big shot.

At the end of my fourth night, I was asked by Helen, the house mom, why I hadn't picked up my "tip outs."

"What the hell is a tip out?"

Helen looked dumbstruck. "Stuart didn't tell you the girls kick back five dollars each for you and the bouncers every night?"

Unbelievable. There were sixty girls in the club at any one time, but at least twenty more came and went during the course of the night. The bouncers stopped by Helen's closet-size office every night for their tribute. She handed me a stack of twenties. "Four days' worth," she said.

Things ran smoothly for the first two weeks. None of the dancers broke any of the rules. I noticed no one making numerous trips to the ladies' room, which would suggest nose candy. None of the women left with customers or passed notes to big spenders. In fact, part of my job was to make certain the dancers weren't hassled when they left the club. I made sure cabs or limos were waiting for them right outside the door.

Stuart was getting impatient. "You mean to tell me these broads aren't doing blow in the jane?"

"That's what I'm telling you."

"And they all leave alone?"

"That's right."

He was pacing the floor, in his office. "Well, we gotta do something about that."

I didn't think I was going to like what I was about to hear. "Like what?"

Stuart went to a bookshelf behind his desk. He selected a thick volume and opened the front cover. The book was hollow. He took out five small glassine envelopes. Reluctantly, he handed them to me. This was his private stash. He tossed me a ring with one key on it. "This is the master to all the lockers. After the place is empty, open a few and spread these around."

I dropped the drugs to the floor. "Who do you think I am, G. Gordon Liddy? I'm not a burglar and I'm sure as hell not going to flake any of these kids." I knew he could easily plant the stuff himself, so I added, "And don't tell me to conveniently find the stuff if you have me search the lockers."

He got smug. "There's an extra thousand in it for you." He reached for his wallet.

"Don't bother. I signed on to catch them if they were doing anything wrong. Well, up till now, they're not. I'm not about to jam up one of these kids for a grand, or ten grand. Forget it." I was hot but controlled. Stuart must have seen the fire in my eyes.

"Okay, okay." He got contrite. "I'll tell you what . . . just be a little more alert. I find it hard to believe I've got over sixty broads here who don't do drugs. I caught dancers all the time in Lauderdale."

Fort Lauderdale ain't New York, I thought. These girls are pulling in thousands of dollars a night, why screw it up for a line of brain buster? They could be blowing their brains out but they weren't doing it at work. "I'll be a regular Sherlock fucking Holmes," I said and left him to his worries.

Two months later things were still going smoothly. I was making more money—steadily—than I had ever made. Three thousand dollars was a bad week for me. Stuart had created a "champagne room" where our best customers were entertained privately. Champagne and hors d'oeuvres were gratis. Hardly anyone drank the champagne even though the club was pouring Cristal. These customers weren't happy unless they spent money. A shot of thirty-six-year-old single malt scotch went for forty dollars. We went through ten bottles a night, more when we got an influx of Japanese businessmen. Stuart put me in charge of the champagne room, figuring that if the girls were going to proposition a customer, they would go after the really wealthy ones. It didn't happen. Did these women attend a Kathie Lee Gifford seminar or what? I've dealt with more corrupt nuns.

While I was making a ton of money doing my original job, my stewardship of the champagne room propelled me into the land of tipping paradise. I actually had a customer who would tip me twenty dollars for telling him the correct time. He asked me at least five times a night. One night I left my house without my watch and was thrown into a panic. I actually sent one of the bouncers to a local Radio Shack for a watch. He came back with a watch that looked like Dick Tracy's two-way wrist radio. It was everything from an altimeter to a barometer. Somewhere in that electronic marvel was the correct time, but I was damned if I could find it. There were more buttons on the watch than in an elevator. I was pushing most of them at once trying to get the time out of the damn thing when Time Guy walked up to me. He had a huge cigar sticking out of his mouth.

"Got the time, Wags?"

I was frustrated with the goddamn watch. "Yeah, twenty-nine point two and falling."

"Thanks." He shoved a twenty in my pocket.

The following night there was a coup d'état. I had gotten to work an hour early, as usual, and was told by Chet that a Mr. McReady wanted to see me.

"Who the hell is Mr. McReady?"

"Our new boss."

Bill McReady turned out to be the promoter Stuart was trying to oust. Apparently, Stuart had been toppled the day before in an out-of-court settlement. McReady was in, Stuart was out. Was I being summoned to get a pink slip?

McReady met me at the bar. He was around forty, and wearing sharply creased jeans, a white silk shirt, and a black silk unconstructed jacket. He smiled and held out his hand. "Bill McReady. You must be Wags."

He was an affable guy. We talked for ten minutes. He had spent seven years promoting topless clubs; he knew the business. He expected the day-to-day operation to remain the same. No, my job wasn't in jeopardy; in fact, I was getting a promotion. He was creating the position of manager, a job Stuart allegedly did himself and for which he drew a salary. My pay doubled, but I lost my billing rate. McReady had no idea I'd been employed as a spy by Stuart. He knew me only as the head of security.

The more things change, the more they remain the same. The club didn't miss a beat. Business as usual. I was wondering if my private investigation days were over. The only job I had had for over three months was at Topsey's. I was turning down all other assignments. Truthfully, I was content to stay where I was. The money was excellent and I didn't have to deal with the con men, philanderers, thieves, and other assorted miscreants I was used to interacting with on a daily basis. Who would have thought that working in a topless club would bring me peace of mind? It never fails that when things seem to be going smoothly, the proverbial monkey wrench appears.

I had spent three violence-free months at the club. Every so often a drunk would have to be removed or a shoving match would have to be nipped in the bud but I hadn't thrown a punch or been threatened since I had been there. When I was on The Job, it was a rare night that went by when I wasn't involved in some sort of physical altercation. Is it any wonder that I found a home in Topsey's?

It was on a Friday night, late even by club standards—about two A.M. Four young guys swaggered in, all in their mid-twenties, all wearing the same uniform: dark suit, no tie, and a black silk shirt. Gold neck chains reflected the club's twinkling bar lights. Wiseguy wanna-bes. The walk was there—a slight bop with nodding head—like one of those German shepherd statues you see perched on the rear decks of cars. They all wore their hair the same way, slicked back and shiny. All they needed were hats and shades to look like the Blues Brothers. If I had to identify them later in court, I'd have a problem. They all looked alike. Their young, cold eyes surveyed the room. I approached them.

"Can I help you?" I asked, staring down the biggest of the lot. Bulging muscles pulled at his jacket button. If I could get a psychological advantage over the biggest guy, I'd have an edge in case there was trouble later.

"Yeah," he said, chewing a chunk of gum the size of my grandson's Play-Doh. "Me and my friends want a table."

"Kitchen's closed," I said. I had yet to blink. Neither had he.

"We're just drinkin'. Got any champagne?" He finally blinked but saved face by looking past me, grinning like a cat, at one of the dancers. The girl turned away, ignoring him. His leer turned to a scowl.

"We serve Cristal mag and rosé," I said. "Five hundred and fifty dollars for the rosé; a hundred more for the mag."

The punk didn't seem impressed. "Yeah, yeah, the mag's good." I had the distinct impression that the last drink he'd consumed with bubbles had been a Pepsi. "Give us a table."

"I'll need a credit card up front," I said, thinking they would never produce a legit card.

Hercules produced an American Express card. "Here, Jeeves, check this out." He smirked. The name on the card ended in a vowel. What a surprise.

I left them standing by the door while I ran the card.

It was good. I had no choice but to serve them. I seated them near the bathroom, then got Chet to stand just inside the main entrance.

"Keep your eye on these guys," I said. "I'll be at the end of the bar within shouting distance." Chet nodded. We assumed our positions.

An hour and a half later, we were getting ready to close. The wanna-bes had consumed three bottles of Cristal mag. They had been a little noisy, but not out of control. They'd made remarks to the waitress, which she had ignored. No one had tried to touch the help. I felt these guys were at the club for a reason. If not to raise hell, then what? I went to their table with the bad news and the charge slip. "Last call, gents, we're closing." I pushed the tray in front of the kid with the card.

They exchanged looks. The blowhard sneered at me. "I ain't signin' it. The service sucked," he said, glancing sideways at his buddies. They all laughed.

I shot a quick glance at Chet. Without taking his eyes off me, he rapped twice on the door behind him. The two bouncers were inside in a second. Chet must have clued them in because they looked like they were itching for a fight. They were at the table in a flash.

We outweighed the four Muttskateers by at least three hundred pounds. The guy sitting opposite the cardholder stood up. He was big, but I was bigger. He moved back his jacket to reveal an automatic in his waistband. Chet, the two other bouncers, and I unbuttoned our coats. We were all armed.

The first image that went through my mind was a scene from the Kevin Costner movie, *Wyatt Earp*. The Earp brothers are facing off the Clanton brothers at the O.K. Corral. They're practically nose to nose. In the movie, it seemed like minutes before someone pulled a gun and fired the first shot. I had a feeling the same thing was about to happen here. The club was almost empty. The few people who remained glanced our way when the one wiseguy stood up. You could have fit all of us into a small closet.

The other three junior Gottis got up. Chests swelled. I admit I was scared; I couldn't see not getting hurt before whatever was about to transpire ended. My throat went dry, a sure sign that the proverbial shit was about to hit the fan. I heard a voice behind me.

"What's going on here?" It was Bill McReady.

I didn't dare take my eyes off the punks. "Our *guests* here refuse to sign the AmEx charge."

"It's okay, Wags. They're my guests. I'll get the check." Now I turned around.

"We've got a twenty-one-hundred-dollar tab here, boss, you still want to—"

He interrupted me and elbowed his way into the cluster. He was smiling, but it was forced. "Yeah, sure, no problem." He put his arm around the shoulders of the punk closest to him. "I know these guys. I'll take care of it." As quickly as it had started, it was over. The wanna-bes walked away with McReady, smirking at us over their shoulders. The boss went behind the bar himself and made them a round of drinks. When I left an hour later, they were still at the bar.

The same group of shitheads came back at least twice a week. I was forced by McReady to be civil to them. It was tough. Every time they showed up, their checks got bigger. They never paid. They topped out at about three thousand dollars a visit. After a while they didn't even bother to call McReady when they were given a bill, they just walked out. I thought it was time me and the boss had a talk. I went to his office one night just before closing.

"Another three-grand check for the party boys, boss," I said as I sat down in front of his desk.

McReady avoided my eyes. "It's okay, they're friends— or friends of friends—you know what I mean."

"You still want me to serve them?" McReady got tight-lipped, but nodded. I got up and began to walk out.

"Wags, hold it a minute, I want to talk to you." Then it all came out.

The punks had said they were emissaries from a Cosa Nostra family. McReady was being pressured to provide them with freebies. So far they had cost the club fifteen thousand dollars.

"One of them came up to me last week," he said. "They want to throw a party here—for fifty people." McReady was sweating. "I can't afford this, Wags. It's bad enough they're banging me for a few grand a week. A party would break me."

I'd seen this happen before. The unpaid checks start small, then they gradually increase. Veiled threats are made. Before you know it, the club's turned into the International House of Grease Balls. "We got two choices . . . actually, three choices," I said. "We could refuse to let them in, call the cops, or my personal favorite."

"Which is?"

"Let them in as usual and insist they pay their bill. If they don't, we use physical force. Call their bluff. These guys could be acting without any backing. They're in their twenties; we're not talking made guys here."

McReady pondered my suggestion. After rubbing his chin for a few seconds, he said, "Nah, I can't take the chance. Someone could toss a firebomb in the place, maybe beat up a customer. I saw it happen to a club uptown. They were out of business in two months." He lowered his voice. "I made some calls. Maybe this thing could be straightened out."

McReady had contacted the local mob boss through an intermediary. He wanted a meeting. The problem could be solved. "Might cost me a few bucks." McReady shrugged. "So what?"

I had no money invested in his business, so it wasn't my place to insist that my way was the right way. He could do what he wanted. "Do what you think is right." I assumed our little talk was at an end. I got up to leave.

"Hold on a second," McReady said. "I'm meeting a guy tomorrow night." He mentioned a restaurant in Greenwich Village. "I want you to go with me. I'll call and say I'm bringing you. You think that'll be a problem?"

I assumed I would be checked out. I shook my head. "Probably not, but what do you need me for?"

"Protection."

For the most part, we choose the way we die. Smokers know that cigarettes will probably kill them. I've been smoking Lucky Strikes since I was thirteen years old. Lung cancer runs in my family. Do I really care? If I did, I'd be an ex-smoker. People with high cholesterol levels still jam their faces with fettuccine Alfredo, what my doctor calls "heart attack on a plate." If people watched their diets, heart disease wouldn't be running rampant.

The day of the meeting with the majordomo wiseguy I knew I was killing myself. Not that sitting down with the mob would cause my heart to stop beating, but I knew that involvement with that element would ensure a downward spiral that would make me wish I was dead. I just felt it in my bones. A cop's instincts are more acute than the average person's. This is why most of us survive a hostile twenty years. To this day, I still can't figure out why I can smell trouble when no one else can. I guess the cop's instinct stays sharp, like a lion on the hunt.

But did I pay attention to my instincts and refuse to go? I'm sure you already know the answer to that. I was there early—the thrill of the kill.

I picked McReady up at the club and headed to a restaurant on Sullivan Street, in the Village. He was nervous and it showed. If he had opened and closed his window one more time, I figured he was planning to jump out of it. We made the trip in silence. There was nothing to rehearse, nothing to go over, no little scenario that we had previously discussed. My boss was going to plead with a perfect stranger for peace in his own business. Welcome to the Big Apple.

The cozy Italian restaurant was empty despite its being well into the dinner hour. There was one man behind the bar. He looked up as we entered. He motioned for us to come over. McReady said the man's name as we walked to where he stood. I kept my mouth shut. Everyone shook hands. Very cordial. The man came from behind the bar. "I'm going to search youse both now, don't be offended," our host said. His demeanor was dour, his voice made Peter Falk sound like a mezzo soprano. He was about sixty, with a full head of silver hair. He was dressed in a dark gray suit, not your usual bartender ensemble. He didn't give his name, I didn't ask. I shrugged and turned to face the bar, assuming the position I had used with many a perp over the years.

"Ex-cop, huh?" Silver said.

"With the emphasis on *ex*," I said. He gave me an expert toss, more concerned about a recording device, I thought, than a gun. I had left my pistol at home. I wouldn't have felt safer in a church. This was a money meeting; it would be cordial. McReady lifted his hands above his head. Silver searched him.

"Okay, sit," Silver said. He pointed to a minuscule table with two chairs. We sat. Our new friend towered above us. "Here's how it's gonna work. See that doorway back there?" He jerked a thumb over his shoulder. He didn't wait for a nod. "You two go through that door. The boss will be in there, sittin' at a table." He looked at McReady. "You know who you're meetin'?"

McReady swallowed hard. "Yeah, Mr.—"

Silver held up a hand as big as a manhole cover. "No names." I had no idea who McReady was supposed to meet. He didn't volunteer the information, I didn't ask. None of my business. "If you recognize him, don't say his name. Understand?"

McReady nodded like a woodpecker. I said, "I'm with him. Can we go in there now?"

"Yeah, sure. I'll be out here," Silver said, a threat more than a statement of fact.

The room in the back was small and dimly lit. It looked like it had once been a kitchen; a metal sink and two refrigerators hugged one wall. A man was seated at a butcher-block table in the center of the room. I recognized him from numerous news stories over the years. He was dressed in baggy sweatpants and a ratty gray sweater. Mr. Big sported at least a three-days' growth of beard. He could have taken some sartorial tips from the muscle guy behind the bar but I wasn't about to suggest it.

This was a powerful man. His name won't be mentioned here because, while he might currently be in jail for the next twenty-seven years, his associates aren't. He was drinking espresso from a dainty cup. There were two chairs next to the table. He looked at both of us for a few seconds.

He pointed to a chair. "You," he said, pointing to McReady, "sit there." He shot me a look. "You can wait outside."

Talk about your wasted trip. McReady looked at me helplessly. "I'll be outside with Smiley," I said. "You're okay." Business would be discussed here, I was certain of that. A man that influential in the mob doesn't attend beatings, only funerals.

The restaurant was still devoid of customers. Something told me that whoever owned the place didn't care if one meatball was ever served in the joint. The bartender stood at his post with his arms folded. He barely gave me a nod when I emerged from the back room.

I'd like to report that he and I had an intellectual discussion about the history of organized crime in America and the current practice of using the RICO statute to put wiseguys away for hundred-year stretches, but he ignored me and I busied myself counting the wine bottles suspended in cute little wicker baskets from the ceiling. Gangsters learn in Wiseguy 101 that cops are either to be ignored or paid off. Friendly banter is frowned upon. I've been frequenting the same Italian restaurant in Queens since I was a rookie. The owner is a captain in the Genovese mob. He never once acknowledged me or the people I brought in with me.

I've been retired several years and he still won't recognize me. All this is fine with me just as long as he keeps turning out that incredible osso buco every Thursday night. If someone had told me that in less than one month my life would depend on mob influence, I would have thought them crazy.

McReady came out of the back room as white as a hunk of mozzarella. He kept his head down, hands in his pockets.

"Let's go," he said as he breezed past me. He sounded weak, defeated.

I didn't press him for a blow by blow when we got in the car. We were about a mile from the restaurant when he turned to me. There was resignation in his face.

"I've got myself a new partner."

chapter twelve

I realized when we got back to the club that it had been a setup all along. Right from the outset, the wanna-bes had been sent to Topsey's by our unkempt friend. This is how things work in New York. It was never expected that McReady would call the police or challenge the mutts head-on. What you do is, you make some phone calls. Call in some favors to help you solve your problem. Eventually, all roads lead to the Big Guy. Could he help? Certainly, not a problem. Come on down, we'll talk.

McReady pleaded his case. The Big Guy considered his problem, then came to the conclusion that he really couldn't help. He wouldn't dirty his hands with such trash. McReady would have to work out the problem himself. Of course, by this time McReady's desperate. If Don Porko here can't help me, he figures, who can? He begins to whine. The don reconsiders. What's in it for him? Within ten minutes, McReady has a new partner. And he *begged* for it.

The mob muscles its way into legitimate business for one of two reasons. One, to make money through the sale of whatever it is the business sells, or two, to "bust it out." A bust-out is conducted with a marginally successful business. In a restaurant or club, for example, the wiseguys come in and start ordering supplies—booze and food—on credit, all charged to the club, which up to this time enjoyed a good credit rating. The supplies come in the front door and go out the back to be sold on the street for a fraction of what they're worth. The mob never pays a bill, and eventually the business is no longer extended credit. The next, and last, phase involves the "fat-fire-in-the-kitchen" scam. A day before the blaze, the joint is cleaned out, every stick of furniture and everything else of value, then torched. The owner collects the insurance money (hopefully), which he dutifully turns over to his "partner."

I didn't think Topsey's would suffer a bust-out. The club was making too much money. For the first few days after McReady's meeting, I expected his new "partner" to come waltzing in with an entourage. McReady was panic-stricken. It didn't take him long to realize he'd been suckered and he wasn't looking forward to sharing the profits with someone whose name he probably couldn't pronounce. But he had no choice. I didn't inquire as to how many points McReady gave away. It was none of my business, but knowing what I know I'd say it was somewhere around 20 percent. The only positive thing to come of all this was that McReady would be immune to the problems that are endemic in New York when you're trying to run a business: private sanitation, health inspectors, union complaints, and anything else that required influence or a six-foot-five late notice.

A week went by. Finally, on the eighth day, one of the bartenders told me my presence was requested upstairs. McReady was in hushed conversation with another man when I walked into the office. I had gotten used to not knocking. The look I got from McReady's friend told me those days were over.

"Wags," McReady said, "I'd like you to meet Frank Black. He just bought into the place." I detected a wince when he said that. "Frank, this is Jimmy Wagner, my manager and security chief." He was trying his best to be cheerful but his grin made him look like he'd caught his finger in a light socket.

Frank Black was in his mid-fifties, a shade under six feet tall, and very well dressed. He was wearing a dark green double-breasted suit, a crisp white shirt, a red-and-green tie, and dark green suede loafers. An old-time cop I worked with once told me that the best way to size up a man is to look at his shoes. If they're well cared for and have heels that aren't worn, then you're dealing with a sharp guy. Actually, the way the old-timer put it was, "If he don't take care of his shoes, then he don't wipe his ass." Words to live by. Black's shoes were brushed clean and had squared-off heels.

McReady's new partner got up to shake my hand, something I didn't expect. His grip was strong, confident; he didn't try to twist my arm off to prove he was a tough guy. His hair was salt and pepper going to all salt, and he stuck to the mob dictum—no facial hair. His face was almost unlined but deeply tanned. "Jimmy," he said, "you're fired." Then he laughed.

McReady was in no mood for a little joke. I thought he was going to have a stroke. His face got red and his eyes bulged. I didn't have time to react other than to give a weak smile.

"I was thinking of going for the operation anyway," I said. "These broads make more money than I'll ever make. What do you think, boss," I said to a hyperventilating McReady, "would you hire me as a dancer if I had tits?" More laughs.

I stayed with them for about an hour. We talked mostly about the business but Frank touched upon his interest in cooking and his knowledge of wine. Normally, McReady wanted me on the floor at all times. *He* would come down to see *me* if he wanted something. Now, it seemed, Frank Black liked my company and I wasn't about to be asked to leave. Finally, I begged off and returned to work.

I didn't know what to make of the new partner. I knew his name wasn't Black; it didn't take Columbo to figure that out. For him to be entrusted with overseeing the mob's new business venture, he had to be a made man and extremely trustworthy. He also had to be an "earner," mobdom's highest accolade. I hate to admit it, but I liked the guy.

Frankie, as he liked to be called, stopped in at least twice a week. He usually came in alone. Occasionally, he showed up with an "associate," always male, and they would huddle in a corner and talk quietly. The young mutts who started it all were never seen again. Frankie also liked to go to the champagne room, smoke Cubans, eat a four-course meal and have two or three girls dance for him. He tipped well, which surprised me. He was in a position to take; he didn't have to give. It was a rare night when he didn't tip me a hundred dollars. But he wasn't all altruism; his checks always came to at least seven hundred dollars and he always signed for them. I'm sure McReady either wrote them off as business expenses or threw them out.

There was no denying that Frankie's presence had brought an increase in business. The club was always jammed, and the lines to get in required at least an hour's wait. I began spending more time with him at his table late at night when things got slow. He told me he had spent his whole adult life "doing what he was doing" and had never done any jail time. He told me he had reached a time in his life where he valued the family—his real family, a wife and two daughters— more than the wild life he had once led. I took most of what he said with the proverbial grain of salt. He was a wiseguy involved in a treacherous lifestyle, although he was, perhaps, a little more polished than the average mobster. I never met a wiseguy who wouldn't laugh with his best friend, then shoot him in the head if so ordered. It's a life of deception and traitorous behavior and I never lost sight of what Frank Black really was. I felt that if Bill McReady ever held back Frank's cut, I'd find out who the real Frank Black was. Still, we got along. We knew who we were.

About two months after Frankie arrived, McReady pulled me over to the side of the bar.

"I don't want you talking to Frankie." He was drunk but hadn't reached the falling-down stage as yet.

"What are you talking about?"

"You know what I'm talking about. This guy moves in and all of a sudden you're buddies. Listen, you're the manager. I don't give a shit if the joint's empty, I don't want you sitting down and talking to anybody, and that includes Frankie." He shot his cuffs and straightened his tie. The boss had spoken.

The last thing I needed was to piss McReady off. He had been good to me and maybe he was right. I had never sat down at a table with anyone before, including McReady. It was time to back off from Frank Black.

Three days later, Frankie ambled in. I was cordial but stayed away. The same thing happened the next two nights he came in. Finally, on the third night he had one of the dancers tell me he wanted to see me. He was alone at his usual table in the champagne room.

"There a problem, Wags?" he said between bites of filet mignon. "You don't stop by anymore, you know, to bullshit and have a drink." His eyes bored into mine. He was looking for a lie.

I wasn't going to lie to the man but I could play it down. "The boss says I'm getting a little too friendly with the customers." I rolled my eyes for effect. "I'm not acting professional enough."

Frankie raised his eyebrows. "Oh, really? Then it's not just me, huh? I mean, Bill isn't complaining because you're spending too much time with me instead of doing whatever the hell you have to attend to at three in the morning, right?"

I assured him that that wasn't the reason. I let him get back to his meal.

Frankie came in the following night, which was rare for him. He usually skipped at least one night. He beckoned me over to the bar.

"Listen, Wags," he said, putting his arm around my shoulders, "I appreciate the fact that you want to protect your boss—" I started to protest. "Uh-uh, don't bullshit a bullshitter," he said. "Me and Billy-boy had a talk. From now on, you can talk to whoever the fuck you want to, me or anybody else. If he says anything, you tell me. From now on, you're fireproof. Got it?"

A classic show of force. Frank Black didn't give a damn if I spent time with him or not. What he wanted to do was show McReady who was really running the place. After that night, I could have pissed in a potted plant and McReady would have had to take it. I wasn't going anywhere.

The last time I was in a bar fight was twenty-five years ago. So much time has passed that I've forgotten how it got started. It probably had something to do with a girl. I remember flailing away at two guys when a pretty brunette came from out of nowhere and tried to break it up. I inadvertently hit her and knocked her out cold. She was rushed to the hospital with a severe concussion. I felt so bad about what I'd done that I visited her in the hospital every day for the week she was there, toting flowers or some other gift. We became friendly . . . very friendly. That woman was Pat, my future wife. We laugh about it now, but at the time I was mortified.

My next bar fight occurred in Topsey's about three months after Frank Black moved in on McReady. This one almost cost me my life.

I don't consider myself a tough guy. When I was on The Job, I got more cooperation out of people by talking to them than by pushing them around. To me, the mark of a bad cop is having to rely on physical force to get compliance on the street. A cop's best weapon is his ability to communicate. There are times, however, when brute strength is the only way to survive.

That night at the club I had to rely on brawn to save

my life. No amount of talking was going to allow me to get home to my family in one piece.

Part of my job at the club entailed checking the bathrooms, which were located in the basement. I was supposed to look for people doing drugs in the stalls or the enterprising burglar who wanted to hide down there until after the club closed. Every so often I would catch some stockbroker doing coke in the men's room. I'd tell him he was finished for the night, and that if I caught him again, he was going to get thrown out of the club. Rarely did I ever catch the same guy twice. The ladies' bathroom was hardly ever used because women rarely came into the club. The dancers had their own lavatory.

Routine leads to complacency. I actually looked forward to checking the bathrooms because it was quiet down there and I wouldn't have to maintain a watchful eye on the dancers to make sure they weren't hassled. I'd usually take fifteen minutes or so, have a smoke, make my rounds, and go back upstairs. For me, it was like a break.

That particular night I had just extinguished what was left of a cigarette and had sauntered into the men's room like I didn't have a care in the world. The room had green marble floors and walls. It reminded me of a mausoleum. It appeared empty. I had started to leave when I heard a sound coming from one of the stalls. It had the unmistakable ring of someone vacuuming a white powdery substance up his nose. Another financial wizard, I thought, blowing his commissions on cocaine. I tried the stall door. Locked.

I rattled the door. "C'mon. Open up—security." I figured I'd hear the toilet being flushed, with that night's marching powder being given a burial at sea. No response.

At first I got a little aggravated, then that quickly changed to concern. What if someone overdosed in there and the snorting sound I'd heard was the last one made before the guy in the stall went into cardiac arrest? If it could happen to that basketball player, Len Bias, it could certainly happen to some out-of-shape Wall Streeter. I gave a few more bangs on the door and went to plan two, which I had just made up.

I went into the adjoining stall, mounted the toilet bowl, and peered over the wall. As soon as I stuck my head into the next stall, I was hit between the eyes by a fist as big as a turkey. The lights went out momentarily and I fell, feet first, into the commode I was standing on. When I regained my senses seconds later, I was standing ankle-deep in toilet water. All I could think about was my four-hundred-dollar Ferragamo shoes that were taking a bath. I was pissed, no pun intended.

I heaved myself out of the water and hoisted myself over the top of the stall. I was met by another punch, this one deflecting off my shoulder. The guy in the stall took up most of it. I got a quick glimpse of a huge white guy in a suit, with short hair, as I sailed over the wall into his space.

We were standing nose to nose trading punches so fast that I must have belted the wall as many times as I hit my opponent. He was so big that he had a tough time bringing back his arms to get the full power behind his punches. At that moment, I was getting the better of him. The only advantage in being so close to each other was that there wasn't enough room for him to knee me in the groin. But I guess that worked both ways. We were cursing and screaming, me in English, him in what sounded like Russian. While he was bloodier than I was, he didn't seem very affected by my blows. I attributed that to the cocaine, which now lay on the floor in a sandwich baggie.

We were about two minutes into the fight and I was getting exhausted. The Russian just lowered his head and fought from a crouch. Then it dawned on me: He wasn't getting his stamina from the coke; this guy was a goddamn boxer! Now I knew that unless we got out of the stall, this guy would beat me to death. The tide was beginning to turn. He was pummeling me with body blows and I was having trouble breathing. My next thought was: Doesn't anybody take a piss around here? If someone came into the bathroom they would see the commotion and get help. If I ever needed the bouncers, I needed them now.

I was in a bear hug, getting the air squeezed out of me, face to face with a foul-breathed, coke-crazed Russian. I was approaching unconsciousness when I boxed his ears. He howled in pain and I rammed his head against the protruding metal coat hook. Blood was squirting everywhere. He pushed backward and we crashed through the door. He fell, and I landed on him hard. At least we were free of the confinement of the stall. I took advantage of my superior position and whaled into his face with everything I had.

I wear an NYPD sergeant's ring. It's one of the gaudiest pieces of jewelry you'll ever see. A miniature sergeant's shield rests on a chunk of fourteen-karat gold and protrudes upward about half an inch. I figured that since I'd spent enough time on The Job to earn it, I was going to get the gaudiest ring I could find. It could also double as a helluva weapon.

With all the punching I was doing, the ring somehow turned around and the shield was being battered against my palm. It hurt. I was on the Russian's chest swinging away when the pain in my hand became a little too much to bear and I leaped off him, kicking him in the head as I departed. His head snapped to the side and he rolled over. I thought I'd killed him. Then, unbelievably, he started to get up. I struggled to my feet and turned the ring around, shield facing out.

We were both covered with blood. The Russian's face was so obscured by the sea of red that I couldn't even tell how old he was. I was feeling faint. Blood—mine or his, I didn't know which—was in my eyes and, mixed with sweat, it burned like hell. Images were beginning to blur. I knew if I blacked out, he would kill me. I didn't even have the strength to call out for help. We lowered our heads and charged each other. I knew I had to get the best of him or I would surely die.

The ring saved my life. While I took a lot of body shots, the Russian was taking the brunt of the ring's blows directly to the nose and forehead. I had the presence of mind to hammer away at the same spot over and over.

His head looked like a cantaloupe that someone had used for batting practice. Finally, he turned his back on me and busted out of the bathroom. He was heading up the stairs to the club with me right behind him.

He broke through the door leading to the restaurant like he was shot out of a cannon, me in hot pursuit. He bellowed like a bull as he crashed into a table occupied by four Japanese businessmen. Their eyes actually went round with shock. All four wound up on the floor while the mad Russian kept trying to get up. He was slipping on his blood and spilled champagne.

He was on his hands and knees when I pounced on him from the rear.

I heard screams from the dancers and more furniture being tossed around the room. Where the hell were the bouncers? My fists were so sore by this time that I started using my elbows to pummel his head. Every time I hit him, I heard a squishing sound. I was certain that I had penetrated his skull, going into his brain. Still, he fought on.

Finally, I felt someone on my back. The bouncers! Wrong.

The Russian had a friend. He had one arm around my neck and was pounding the back of my head with his fist. I held on to the first Russian like he was trying to get away with my winning lottery ticket. We were wedged together like that for seconds but it seemed like hours. I was the meat in a psycho sandwich.

I felt the guy on top of me loosen his grip. The air went out of him. Chet, I found out later, had kicked him in the ribs, breaking six. The other two bouncers separated us. It was over.

The police were called. Because I was a retired sergeant, the first cops on the scene called a lieutenant off patrol to investigate the disturbance. He wanted to know if anyone wanted to make a formal complaint. The Russian was being strapped to a gurney on his way out the door. He was lucid but not talking. His buddy gasped a weak no and declined medical attention. Later we would learn he wound up in a hospital in Brooklyn because one of his broken ribs had punctured a lung. McReady, my boss, spoke for me: No complaints at this time. If the Russian wanted to make something of it later, we would file cross complaints. The cops did their usual paperwork and departed.

I was groggy and in much pain. One of the dancers asked me what hurt. I pointed to the back of my knee, "This is the only part that *doesn't* hurt." McReady insisted that I go to the hospital. Chet commandeered one of the limos outside and we went to Beth Israel Hospital, less than a mile away. I was stretched out on a gurney right next to the Mad Russian. Two ER doctors were working feverishly to stop his bleeding. He was floating in and out of consciousness. I found out later that he took seventy-two stitches to the head. He had also lost seven teeth. Looking at him stretched out, I wondered how the hell I'd won the fight. The man was huge—at least three inches taller than me. His knuckles were a mass of scar tissue. Thank God for my ring.

Did I say I won the fight? I had a dislocated shoulder, a sprained right wrist, a broken nose, and a ruined tuxedo. Not exactly a draw, and I knew I'd be hurting for a while.

The next morning, I literally could not get out of bed. I love those PIs on television who get beaten with chair legs and manage to get laid, all in under an hour. I knew I'd be a wreck for a while. My wife panicked and wanted me back in the hospital. I refused. I was suffering from intense soreness and pain but I would live. All I would get at the hospital was painkillers. I had a fistful from the previous night. I bore the discomfort. Each day, it diminished a bit more. By day three, I was able to get out of bed without grimacing. By the end of the first week, I was doing mild stretching exercises.

McReady was good. He called at least once a day to

check up on me. I could take all the time off I needed, he said, just get better. After nine days, the tape was off my nose, the black eyes were healing nicely, and I was ready to go back to work. About three hours before I was to leave for the drive into Manhattan, Bill McReady appeared at my door. I knew we had a problem.

I introduced him to my wife. We sat down for coffee and made small talk but I knew he wanted to get me alone. Pat sensed it too.

"I'll leave you guys to yourselves for a while." She gave me a concerned glance as she left the room.

"Wags," McReady said, obvious concern in his voice, "you can't come back to the club."

This I never expected. All I could ask was, "Why?"

"The Russian, Wags, he's mobbed up. He's been making threats. I've been getting calls."

"What kind of calls?" I wasn't concerned yet, just contemplating my next move.

"That you're gonna get whacked as soon as you come back to work. I can't take a chance on you getting killed."

"Killed?" Now I was concerned.

"His name's Boris, Wags. He's an enforcer for the Russian mob in Brooklyn. Bad people. He says he's gonna kill you. I believe him."

The Russians have their own version of the Mafia. They're more violent than the Italian faction ever dreamed of being. They're strangers in a foreign country, the new kids on the block. To get a foothold in organized crime, they control through excessive violence. You slight a Russian mobster, he kills you, your wife and kids, the family dog, and the neighbors. Now I was scared.

McReady would tell the Russians that I wasn't coming back. Just doing that would put him in jeopardy but he didn't seem too concerned. After all, what was he paying Frankie Black for? He said he would have Frankie call me. He suggested that in the meantime, I move my family out of the house.

I have a sister in New Jersey. She's married to a cop, and we've been going to their house in rural Monmouth County for years. It was the start of the summer vacation for the kids. Pat didn't like it, but the family was going there for an extended vacation until I worked out the problem.

They were gone the next day. I followed them in my car as far as the Outerbridge Crossing to make sure they weren't being followed. Once I was certain they weren't, I went back home and waited for the phone to ring. I busied myself with cleaning my guns.

The next day, Frankie called.

"Deep shit, kid," he said.

A classic understatement. He was careful about what he said over the phone but he did tell me that he had had time to check out Boris. The Mad Russian turned out to be just that—a fucking nut. He had been arrested for two murders in Brooklyn and had beaten both charges. There was also a string of assault collars, including one for beating up a priest who had backed into his car. And Boris had been in this country for only five years. He had been granted political asylum. I should be so lucky.

Frankie told me that he would "see some guys" on my behalf. He didn't guarantee anything. "These fucking guys are crazy," he said. "They listen to who they want to listen to." He would be in touch. Wonderful.

I vegetated in the house for three weeks. I was going

nuts. My family called several times a day. The kids wanted to come home. All this and I was running out of money. I had to do something to keep busy. Calls were coming in almost daily with opportunities to work. I was turning all of them down.

At the end of my third week of captivity, I reevaluated my situation. A few years ago I had been a cop, a good cop. I had locked up the kind of animal who was hunting me today. Now I found myself holed up in my own home, window shades drawn, two .45 automatics locked and loaded. I hadn't shaved in a week. Every time the phone rang, I jumped. Every little noise sent me scurrying for my guns. I took showers with an automatic in a plastic baggie. What had I become? I decided then and there that if the Russians wanted me, they could come and get me. Fuck them. I was resuming my life.

My first job as a hunted man was providing security for Mariah Carey's wedding. At that time, she was the hot entertainer of the week and her engagement to her mentor, Tommy Mottola, had been in all the gossip columns when it was announced. The wedding was certain to be a security nightmare. Pictures of the happy couple could probably bring thousands of dollars. I met with Tommy Mottola's "people." They wanted a quiet ceremony and reception. I liked the idea of quiet; the last thing I wanted to do was attract attention.

The ceremony was held in a church on Fifth Avenue, in Manhattan. The bride was beautiful (did I have to mention that?). Everybody who was anybody showed up: Tony Bennett, Billy Joel, Bruce Springsteen, Tony Danza—the list of celebrities was endless. Security was extremely tight. I was just one of thirty former cops and federal agents assigned. We formed three impenetrable rings around the church and the building where the reception was held. Each ring of men was its own security. Whoever wanted to gain access had to pass through three separate checkpoints.

We had some problems in the church as we were leaving. Paparazzi from all over the world jockeyed for position to get "the shot." We didn't let them get too close. We were mostly concerned about the lone nut who wanted to get his version of "the shot." Mark David Chapman was on everybody's mind. If it could happen to John Lennon, it could happen to Mariah Carey. But except for some pushing and shoving, everything went off without a hitch.

The reception was held at the Metropolitan Club. It was hermetically sealed. A gnat couldn't have gotten past us without an invitation. Two hundred and twenty-five guests arrived and every one of them was quickly cleared and admitted. I must have been approached a dozen times by photographers hoping to get inside. Bribe attempts abounded, all of which I turned down. The most I was offered was five hundred dollars.

I was a nervous wreck. More than one former cop asked me if I was feeling okay. I checked myself out in a mirror and saw a ghost. Circles surrounded eyes sunken from lack of sleep. My skin had a pallor from too many days indoors. A new tuxedo I'd ordered just after the fight at the club hung on me. I had a headache from trying to watch everyone at once. Could someone standing in line waiting to be admitted to the reception be a Russian hit man? These people didn't care if they whacked you in front of the director of the FBI, let alone a small army of photographers. I was going to be glad when the day was over.

About an hour into the reception a reporter from the *Daily News*, A. J. Benza, showed up. A.J. had just started writing a gossip column for the paper. He told me that if he could get some quotes from the guests, it would make him look good to his editor.

I owed A.J. a favor. When I was just starting out as a private investigator, he'd written a story on me that was published in a true-crime magazine. It had helped give my career a kick start. Now he sought me out. But I'll give him credit: He never threw the story he did about me in my face. A.J. had a reputation as being a wild man—good with the ladies and an inveterate partier—but he was always a gentleman. I decided to sneak him in.

Right then I should have realized that I had slipped the self-destructmobile into first gear. What the hell was I thinking? If I was caught smuggling A.J. into the reception, my career would be over. I guess that between the Russian mob after me and my exhausted state I just didn't give a damn. This was the first step toward the inevitable meltdown.

I gave A.J. a security button and he mingled with the guests, supposedly doing his job as a bodyguard. He was just starting out then; no one knew he was a gossip columnist. The following day, when the story appeared with direct quotes from some of the attending celebrities, Tommy Mottola's office knew that there had been either a lapse in security or that one of the bodyguards had intentionally admitted A.J. They guessed it was the latter. Accusations abounded. No one ever found out it was me. At least not until now. A.J. went on to become a celebrity in his own right with the hottest gossip column in New York and a regular gig on the E! Channel and *Geraldo!*. I'm sure the Mariah Carey wedding story didn't hurt his career.

I did such a wonderful job for Mariah Carey that someone made a call and recommended me for security on the movie *Carlito's Way*, with Al Pacino, which began shooting in New York shortly after the wedding. I had been getting a few hang-up phone calls at home and I was as jittery as ever. The Russians might stalk me for months before making their move. I hadn't heard from Frank Black. For all I knew, he was jerking me around with his offer to help me get the Russians off my back. A few weeks out of the house working sixteen-hour days sounded good to me. It might take my mind off being assassinated. Movie security is an easy gig; I'd done it several times.

Of course, it turned into a nightmare.

The production company was doing some outdoor shooting in Greenwich Village. There was a scene on a basketball court off Sixth Avenue that was shot during the afternoon and attracted hundreds of people trying to get a glimpse of Al Pacino. It was a security monstrosity. I positioned myself inside the court, and had to keep trespassers away. There were at least a dozen retired cops and security types pulling perimeter security outside the chain-link fence. Somehow, one lone junkie managed to get through.

The hophead was an emaciated bag of bones. What possible problem could this character cause? I asked myself. I politely asked him to leave. He responded by taking a roundhouse swing at me, in the process, falling on his ass.

Now, any other time I would have gotten him in a bear hug and ushered him away, particularly in front of a few hundred witnesses. But I was in my I-don't-give-a-damn mode. I slipped the self-destruct vehicle in second gear, waited for the bum to get up, and hauled off and slugged him. I hit him so hard that he bounced off the fence, which was at least ten feet away, and rebounded back to where I was standing, collapsing at my feet. The crowd began to boo me. Objects were thrown. Six retired cops came to my rescue. A few of us picked the junkie up and ejected him, into the gutter. I went for a cup of coffee, assuming that when I got back the furor would be over.

New Yorkers have short memories. I got back from my thirty-minute exile and everything seemed normal. The crowd was just as big but no one gave me a second glance. Just as I was bending down to scurry under a police barricade, a young uniformed cop tapped me on the shoulder.

"Sir, can I have a word with you?"

The officer was short and skinny. His gun belt was loose and could have used a set of hips to rest on. He didn't even look like he shaved yet. Standing next to him was the junkie I had hit. He was holding a soiled rag to his mouth. It was saturated with blood.

Oh, boy, I thought, here's trouble. "Yes, Officer," I said, trying to sound innocent.

The cop cleared his throat. "Mr. Garcia here says you assaulted him." His voice cracked.

Mr. Garcia. The last time anyone had addressed him as Mr. was probably at an arraignment. The junkie was nodding his head. He pointed at me. "That's the motherfucker hit me, man. Cocksucker, I beat your fuckin' head in, man." But he didn't make a move.

I smiled. "Look, Officer, I'm retired from The Job. We're doing security for the movie. Shithead here was trespassing and took a swing at me. He had to be forcibly ejected, that's all. Now, if you'll excuse me, I've gotta get back inside the court." I turned and the cop touched my arm.

"I'm sorry, sir, but I'm going to have to place you under arrest. Mr. Garcia is lodging a complaint. I have no choice." He reached behind him to get his handcuffs.

I couldn't believe what was happening. Was this the new breed of cop the mayor was so proudly touting? If it was, I was glad I was retired. The junkie couldn't believe it either. He was standing there with his mouth open. "Could we have a few words, Officer?" I took two giant steps backward. The cop followed. He was all ears. "Listen," I said in a low voice, "maybe you didn't hear me . . . I'm retired from The Job. *Retired from The Job*. Get it? When did you get out of the academy?"

"Uh, two months ago, sir."

I looked at his name tag. "Well, Officer Blount, didn't anyone tell you in the academy that junkie complainants are always full of shit? It's a rule, you know. Another rule, Officer Blount, is that you don't lock up a retired cop over a bullshit beef on the say-so of a crackhead. Now, if I were you, I'd walk away and let dickhead over there bitch all he wants to. You just couldn't find me. Thanks." I turned yet again to leave.

"I'm sorry, sir, but I'm going to have to place you under arrest." He waved the cuffs in front of my face.

No more Mr. Nice Guy. "Officer," I said, "you put those cuffs away or I'm going to shove them up your ass." Now I'm threatening cops. Good career move.

The young man turned bright red. He started stuttering and stammering. "I'm . . . I'm gonna get my lieutenant. You st . . . stay right here." He yanked a portable radio from his belt.

This has to be a dream, I thought. "So long, kid," I said. This time I *did* walk away. I didn't get three steps before I heard him yell into the radio, "Ten-thirteen! Ten-thirteen!"

A signal ten-thirteen, for those of you who don't watch *NYPD Blue,* is a distress call from a cop who is in desperate trouble. I'm talking a life-or-death situation, not the bullshit altercation with which I was involved. I looked over my shoulder. The cop was shouting his location into the radio. Almost immediately, I heard the sirens. Cops come from everywhere when they hear a ten-thirteen. The way the idiot cop sounded, you would have thought Jeffrey Dahmer was chewing on his leg.

I had a split second to make a decision: Do I stick around and try to talk myself out of the predicament or do I take off? The logical thing would have been to remain calm, stay put, talk to a seasoned boss, and iron things out. But of course I wasn't thinking very clearly. I threw the self-destruct vehicle into third gear and bolted.

I had one thing going for me: The cops didn't know who I was. The junkie, I was sure, wasn't going to hang around to make certain justice was served. The movie people, I knew, wouldn't want to get involved. They had a picture to shoot. There were fifty thousand retired cops, no one would bother with a photo array. Believe it or not, I had to stay hidden on the floor of the backseat of my car for the rest of that night's shoot. A production-company van had me blocked in. Every so often I'd poke my head up and see a radio car or some foot cops stopping people on the street and asking questions.

I may have been uncomfortable, but I had time to think. First the Russians, now the police. I wasn't part of *us* anymore, I was part of *them*. I was as far removed from my former life as a professional law-enforcement officer as I could ever think of being. I felt like I had never been part of the fraternity. My life was a shambles. My family was in Jersey and I was hiding in the backseat of a Buick. I wouldn't have been surprised if the junkie I'd belted and I had wound up sharing a refrigerator carton under the Williamsburg Bridge.

On top of all this aggravation, my beeper was going off every ten minutes and I had no way of getting to a phone. (My wife had taken the cellular.) Finally, around nine P.M., the van that was blocking me in pulled away. I drove to a phone in an adjoining precinct. The phone number on my beeper was unfamiliar.

"Jimmy Wagner here," I said, my head buried in the phone kiosk. I felt like I was in *The Fugitive*.

"Wags, for Christ's sake, I've been beeping you for five hours." It was Frankie Black. My heart started racing.

"Frankie, I'm sorry. I got jammed up. It's a long story, but it's okay now." I knew these guys didn't like to be ignored. I remembered hearing a tape of John Gotti ordering someone's execution because he missed a meeting. All I needed was for Frankie to be pissed at me too. Not a very exclusive club. I'd have to become a Hare Krishnaer.

"Yeah, well . . . okay," Frankie said. "Don't talk too

much, just listen. I took care of your little problem. You know what I'm saying?" Christ, these people were more paranoid than cops when it came to phones, I thought.

"I'm in the clear?" I asked. Music to my ears. Something was finally going right.

"Tonight. It took some doing, but I sat down with the head muckety-muck. I've got assurances. It's over."

If Frankie had been there with me, I would have kissed him. "I can't say—"

"That's right," he said good-naturedly, "you can't say. At least not on the phone. There's a coupla things, though."

Uh-oh. "What?" I was wondering how many thousands his intervention was going to cost me. I wondered what my life was worth. After a brief contemplation, I was relieved. But at this point, not much.

"First," Frankie said, getting down to business, "no more club. You're out. Part of the deal." He stopped. I heard the distinctive sound of a cigar being torched. I could live with not working at Topsey's. After the fight, the place had lost its appeal.

"What's the other thing?" I asked.

"You owe me a favor."

Fourth gear.

chapter thirteen

About a week later, McReady called me at home to tell me he had some severance money for me. He sounded a helluva lot cheerier than when I'd last spoken to him.

I stopped by Topsey's on a Friday night. It was packed, as usual. My replacement, a swarthy-looking thirty-something, shoved an envelope at me before I could get past the lobby.

"McReady around?" I asked, perusing the darkened room. I was looking for a familiar face. The bouncers had been replaced. The trio on the door were definitely not former law enforcement, unless it was by way of Danamora. The guy who had my job was stereotypically mob.

"He's busy," he said, "but wants you should keep in touch." I detected a slight sneer.

I stuffed the envelope in my pocket and left. Frankie had used my problem with the Russians to put his people in the club. He was going for total control. The way I saw it, I didn't owe him a damn thing. He had smoothed things out for me, but he'd gotten me out of the club as part of the deal. He probably told McReady that the Russians wanted me out. Whatever, I'm sure Frankie didn't know the meaning of quid pro quo. I wasn't looking forward to the day when the phone would ring and it would be Frankie asking me for a favor.

I spent the next few weeks with my family. School was still out and I hadn't had any real quality time with my kids since starting at the club. My wife and I went out to dinner and a movie a few times a week. It felt good to get away from my business and relax. Besides, my injuries weren't entirely healed and I was still waking up as sore as hell.

My mornings were spent in the gym pumping iron and stretching. I've been working out most of my adult life and look forward to my morning gym sessions. I had been a member of the same gym for years and had seen the same faces every morning. One of those faces belonged to Willie Gonzalez.

Willie was a former New York City corrections officer and an avid bodybuilder. He had won some major competitions, including the amateur Mr. Universe contest. He was about forty-two and in phenomenal shape. We talked a lot about a variety of subjects, mostly those dealing with weight training. Once he let slip that he'd quit corrections to become a bodyguard and had just come back from California where he'd spent some time guarding Damon Wayans. Twice he'd appeared in TV skits with Homey the Clown. He was currently working for "the union." He didn't elaborate and I didn't pursue it. He knew what I did but never pressed me for details. I offered him the same courtesy.

After I'd been out of the club for a few weeks, he made me an offer I couldn't refuse.

"You working?" he asked after I had completed a set of bench presses.

I told him I'd taken the summer off to be with my family.

"I've got something that might interest you." He guided me out of earshot of the other gym rats. "I'm working for the First District Council of Carpenters, bodyguarding the president, Fred Devine. Ever hear of him?" I told him I hadn't. "The job's good, pays well, and they take good care of me. Him and the first vice president, John Abbatemarco, go to Atlantic City every now and then. Usually they go alone, you know, to meet with other union people, party a little, like that. They're going on Friday and want security. I've got Devine. I've also got a partner, but he'd be a dud as a bodyguard. Mr. Rogers looks more intimidating. The guys don't care for him very much. I was wondering if you would come with me and look after Abbatemarco."

"Why all of a sudden do they need security?"

"There were some sensitive firings at the Javits Center for some union infractions. I don't really know the specifics; it's not my job. But a couple of the people who got bounced might have some mob connections. Hard to believe, huh?" Willie smiled. "They're a little concerned. Interested?"

"Your partner won't mind?"

Willie shook his head. "He's Mr. Inside. He'd much rather be playing with the books and taking clients to dinner. I'm Mr. Outside."

I discussed the job that night with my wife. The kids' summer vacation was coming to a close and there was that ominous tuition bill due any day. I could have taken a few more weeks off, but we agreed that it seemed like an easy gig. I called Willie that night and told him I'd do it.

John Abbatemarco turned out to be a sweetheart. He was a streetwise guy who'd worked his way up from the bottom of the labor pile to the prestigious position he now held. He had an easygoing manner and we hit it off immediately. Freddy Devine, Willie's guy, looked and sounded exactly like Humphrey Bogart. It was uncanny. I closed my eyes and I was in Rick's Café in *Casablanca*.

Actually, we were in a hotel in Atlantic City. Devine and Abbatemarco were together in union meetings most of the day. They were very good friends but at night they went their separate ways, each schmoozing with different union factions or gambling. Abbatemarco was known as "Johnny Abbadaba." He was a compulsive gambler. He'd bet on anything and almost always lost. He reminded me of a character in the movie *A Bronx Tale*, Eddie Mush. Mush lost every bet he ever made. Anytime he went to the track with his friends, his buddies would tear up their tickets before the end of a race if Mush had bet on their horse. This was the kind of reputation that Abbadaba had. His favorite game was knock rummy. He would play anytime, anywhere. He always had a deck of cards with him and it was normal for him to play a few hands in the limo on his way to a meeting. I once even saw him deal a hand in a slow elevator. He lost to whoever he played against. If he went head to head with Stevie Wonder, I'd bet my kids' college tuition on Stevie.

The AC trip lasted a few days. I figured I had gotten

all the business that I was going to get and I was surprised when Abbatemarco asked me if I'd like to stay on as his bodyguard. I accepted.

I would pick him up at his home in Bensonhurst every morning before sunrise. In addition to his position as first vice president, he was also the business agent for local 257. It's a business agent's job to give out union work to members. Workdays begin early and we were usually on the road by five-thirty A.M. Abbatemarco figured that if he was going to get clipped by some disgruntled ex-employee with mob connections, he'd get it leaving his house, when it was dark. A classic mob killing time. We spent a lot of time together in cars driving to various meetings and union offices. In addition to playing knock rummy when we were stuck in traffic, we had plenty of time to talk.

"You know, Wags," he told me on more than one occasion, "Freddy's gonna step down in a year. He's retiring. Freddy deserves a rest, he's been at this union thing for thirty years." He would poke me in the side. "You know who he's gonna make the new president?"

"Who?" I'd ask for the twentieth time.

"Me," Abbadaba would say, beaming. "That Freddy, he's like a brother to me." He had aspirations of one day heading the International Brotherhood of Carpenters in Washington, D.C.

I didn't see much of Freddy Devine and Willie. Occasionally we would all go out of town on business. We went to Pittsburgh once and the four of us spent evenings together. Freddy and Abbadaba were like family, each could finish the other's sentences. I liked the work because there was no pressure or danger. There were no threats from the fired union workers. The Russian episode seemed far behind me, and I was going to work, like a businessman, every day. Sometimes I had to remind myself to bring a gun.

It seemed like Abbadaba and the union officials had unlimited expense accounts. No one went anywhere unless they traveled by limo. Meals were taken in the best restaurants; only the finest hotels were booked. Wherever the union big shots went, Willie and I went. It was a good life. The membership paid for all of it.

The only glitch in this utopia was Alice, or as she was called behind her back, Fat Alice. While Willie and I were working with the carpenters, he had a side gig doing security work for the Teamsters. Fat Alice was in charge of the Teamsters' local benefits fund and as nasty a person as you'd ever want to meet. Somewhere between forty and fifty, Alice controlled the office like Ma Barker. I would often meet Willie at the Teamsters' downtown office and she would be hollering and swearing at any- and everyone within earshot. Sometimes I'd be stuck waiting for Willie and I'd have to listen to Fat Alice's tirades. While her official title was "head of the benefits fund," she actually ran the office. No one was safe from her sarcasm and bursts of temper. Normally I would have told Alice where to go, but she was an extremely valuable asset to the Teamsters and as an outsider I didn't want to piss her off. If she walked, Willie told me, the Teamsters' hierarchy wouldn't even know where the checkbooks were. She was also privy to the day-to-day financial shenanigans for which unions are famous. So I was polite and held my tongue even though I felt like giving her a hip check out the window on a few occasions.

One morning I went to the Teamsters' office to pick up Willie for an early appointment with Freddy and Abbadaba. The office was crawling with cops. My first thought was that someone had gotten hit. It was worse—at least as far as the Teamsters were concerned. Fat Alice was charging the union president's bodyguard, an ex-cop, with rape. If it was true, I thought, it had to be a blind ex-cop. The place was littered with private security; most union officials have their own guards, something that was a bit of a status symbol. You know: "My bodyguard is tougher than your bodyguard."

The Teamsters did everything to appease her. She wanted justice and they were afraid that if she wasn't happy, she might start talking to the newspapers, or worse, the law. When she wasn't working, she was eating. Or complaining about men. She was divorced— what a surprise—and hated men, at least that's what she said. I think she may have had the hots for the retired cop and he wouldn't give her a tumble. She got back at him with the rape charge. The retired cop vehemently denied laying a hand on her. His case went to a grand jury, just on her complaint. Shortly after the former cop was led away, she demanded bodyguards. Willie was owed a few weeks' vacation from Freddy and took the time off to guard Fat Alice.

"What, are you out of your mind?" I said, amazed that he would give up a gentleman like Freddy Devine for Lucretia McEvil.

Willie shrugged. "Why the hell not? I get a vacation with pay and the Teamsters pay better than Freddy. I'll do my three weeks and go back to Freddy when I'm done." It made no sense to me, but if he could put up with Fat Alice, all the more power to him.

If I were Willie, I'd be fantasizing about plotting the perfect murder. I ran through my repertoire of guns, knives, and exotic poisons and decided on a fiendish, yet diabolical idea. I would steal Fat Alice's Twinkies—she kept a supply in her desk drawer—which would force her to commit suicide. I reminded myself to bounce my idea off Willie.

I continued to watch over Abbadaba. Three weeks went by quickly. I called Willie to break his chops. "Fat Alice drive you nuts yet?" I asked. He took me seriously.

"She's not bad, Wags. Turned out to be a decent lady."

I could make a million dollars with the drugs Willie must have been using. "I think you need to double up on the Prozac, my friend."

"Won't need to. It's over. The grand jury voted no bill on the cop about an hour ago. They refused to indict for the rape. He's cut loose. I'll be back tomorrow." He didn't sound too thrilled.

Fat Alice went ballistic when she got the news that her alleged rapist hadn't been indicted. I heard that she threw furniture around for twenty minutes before security ejected her from the building. Then she quit. The Teamsters, I was sure, were relieved that she went of her own accord. I assumed the saga of Fat Alice was over.

Wrong again.

Everything was back to normal. A few weeks went by. Freddy Devine was getting close to his self-imposed retirement and Abbadaba was buoyant. Soon he would be president and he promised that he would appoint me to a responsible position within the union as soon as he was sworn in. Life was good. By this time

I should have realized what that meant: impending disaster.

Three months before Freddy was supposed to retire, he changed his mind. He decided to stay. Forever. They would have to carry him out feet first for him to leave the presidency, he said. Abbadaba flipped out. He and Freddy exchanged words. They went from being the best of friends to being bitter enemies. Battle lines were drawn, loyalties demanded. I wound up in the Abbadaba camp, Willie with Freddy. Then Abbadaba decided to challenge Freddy for the presidency in the upcoming election.

The election was to be the first popular-vote election in the union's history. Both sides predicted victory. Abbadaba wanted me to work with him on his election strategy.

"I need you on my team, Wags," he said. "Only one problem—I can't pay you." Union rules strictly prohibited using union funds for campaign purposes. He had been good to me; I felt I owed him. And there was the promise of a union job should he win. I climbed on board.

Abbadaba got trounced. His loss made Walter Mondale's drubbing in '84 seem like a squeaker. As soon as we got the news, I started cleaning out my desk. Abbadaba was out of the building in less than an hour, his career over. I was certain that Freddy would clean house and get rid of all Abbadaba's supporters. As I was carting my stuff to the elevator, I ran into Willie.

"Don't go anywhere just yet, Freddy wants to see you."

Freddy greeted me like a long-lost son. Hugs, cheek kisses, the whole bit.

"Wags, I want you to stay."

I was confused. "Why? I supported John."

"Yeah, but at least you showed some loyalty, even if it was to him. All my so-called union brothers were making secret deals with John should he win. I got some calls from *his* people when they thought they were on a sinking ship. You were one of the few people I never heard from. I like that."

What he said was true. There had been a lot of treachery going on. No one had wanted to lose their cushy positions and go back to hammering nails. Everybody in the office had been playing both sides of the game. I had owed my loyalty to John Abbatemarco and he had gotten it. Abbadaba was now gone and I had been ready to accept my fate stoically.

There are two things in life in which I believe strongly, the first being loyalty. It's a trait by which I judge people and one by which I wish to be judged. On the way to Freddy's office, I flashed back to my former partner, Richie Innes. I think of Richie when I think of things I have done in my life that have greatly enriched my sense of well-being and have made me realize that loyalty has its own rewards.

Richie was my radio-car partner for seven years when we were in uniform in the Ninth Precinct. Block for block, the Ninth was the most prolific killing ground in the city. The smallest command in Manhattan, it boasted one of the highest homicide rates in the late seventies, early eighties: fifty bodies a year, on average. Richie and I worked Alphabet City, the precinct's worst area. (The station house and neighborhood were used for exterior shots in *Kojack* and *NYPD Blue*.)

Richie was a big guy—six-three—with a great sense

of humor. He always had me laughing for the entire eight-hour tour. Richie wore reading glasses; not uncommon. In his eighth year on The Job, however, his eyesight became increasingly worse. Within six months he was only able to see shadows directly in front of him and nothing more than fifteen feet away. He was diagnosed as having Pars Planitis, a degenerative eye disease that usually burns itself out before it does too much damage. In Richie's case the disease got progressively worse. His doctor declared him legally blind. He was told that a series of operations, over an eighteen-month period, might restore his sight but that it was a crap shoot. The only problem was that The Job would have retired him as unfit for duty if he had made his illness known. The NYPD rule is that if a cop has under ten years' service and has a debilitating illness, he or she gets retired on one-third pay. Richie had eight and a half years in. With a wife and three young kids, he couldn't afford to leave The Job. He and I decided to hide his blindness. No one but the two of us and the precinct PBA delegate knew of Richie Innes's problem. We had eighteen months to hide it from The Job before he could get the first in a series of operations.

At the beginning, I drove the radio car and he did the paperwork. He insisted on doing part of the driving but quickly changed his mind when he drove his Volkswagen bug into a ten-foot-deep Con Ed excavation in the precinct. A bunch of kindly hookers called the police and the responding cops got a tow truck and pulled him out. After a while he had trouble doing the paperwork even with the aid of a magnifying glass so big it could have doubled as a tennis racket.

Darkened hallways were the worst, and we spent a

lot of time in them. Richie would have his nose practically pressed up against my back when we went up stairs. Bright streetlights were another problem. They looked to Richie like they were exploding sparklers. Sometimes his depression would get to me. We would park in an alley to take a break and he would lament that he would never see his kids grow up. His children were his life and he doted on them. I put myself in his place. The thought of never seeing my kids laugh, or being unable to recognize their troubled teenage expressions, tortured me. I would often make an excuse to leave the car because I would get too upset.

Richie was a smart guy, I mean, really bright. He was frustrated that he couldn't study for the upcoming sergeant's exam. We made a deal. I would read him all the department memos, patrol-guide changes, interim orders, and all the other required paper that contributes to the forward movement of any big city PD. While I read this mountain of paper to him he would close his eyes, lean his head back in the radio car, and soak it all in. He eventually took the test with the aid of his enormous magnifying glass. Richie passed the sergeant's exam. In fact he scored better than me. It would still be years before a list was promulgated, and now all we were concerned about was making sure he kept The Job.

Just when he was about to go over the ten-year mark we handled a family dispute on the top floor of a tenement on Avenue A. By now we had the system down: I led the way up the stairs with Richie right behind me. Once in the apartment Richie was okay and handled the job single-handedly. He didn't need his eyes to calm even the most agitated person. While we were in the apartment a fire started on the first floor.

By the time we were alerted by screaming tenants the hallways were enveloped in blinding smoke. Richie led the entire top floor to safety by feeling his way down the stairs. He remembered what the walls felt like on the way up.

The other thing I believe strongly in life about? What goes around comes around.

We pulled it off. For eighteen months no one had any idea that Richie Innes was blind. The day after he turned ten years on The Job he went sick and had a series of four eye operations spread out over two years. Today he has twenty-five years on The Job and is a lieutenant working in Queens. His sight isn't 100 percent but with special contact lenses and thick glasses it's greatly improved.

I was brought back to the present by a smiling Freddy Devine.

"I've got a new job for you, and for Willie, if you guys want it. I need you to go after the contractors that haven't been keeping up with their union health-and-welfare fund payments." He explained that contractors were obligated to contribute a certain amount of money to a carpenter's health-and-welfare account. A contractor who did very little work with the union would sometimes renege on these payments. Legally, the union could put liens on the businesses and, in extreme cases, get personal judgments against the owners of the companies. "You interested?" I told him I'd think about it. First I needed to discuss it with Willie.

Willie and I went for lunch in Chinatown. He needed me involved because I had a private investigator's license and I had the experience to seek out hidden assets. It turned out that his old partner, Mr. Inside—the one who liked to do the books—liked to do them because he was keeping two sets. He stole thousands from Willie before he was found out. When he got the boot he took his license with him. Willie wasn't eligible for a PI license due to lack of police investigatory experience. Willie needed a new partner who had a private investigator's license. I had kept myself relatively free of trouble since getting into the PI business. One of the reasons for this was that I worked alone—no partners. I could have broken that rule but I didn't entirely trust Willie. He was secretive. I always felt he was working some sort of angle. I came back with a counteroffer.

"Okay, we'll work off my license, but I don't want a share, I want a salary—two thousand a week plus a car. Caddies look nice this year. I also don't want to attend meetings you might have with Freddy. We do the job, I get paid, you do whatever you want with the money that's left." This was a great deal for Willie. While things might start slow, once they got going he could be making a lot of money. Willie agreed, we shook hands, and I got stuck with the lunch check. An omen.

We formed a company called W. G. Brandon, for no reason other than that it sounded nice. I decided to devote as little time as possible to this new venture. A few times a week we would get the name of a business that owed money to the union. The arrears would average about $50,000 for the small companies. Willie and I would pay the owner a visit, spend maybe ten minutes with the guy, and if he paid us, great. If not, we'd go after his bank accounts.

There was a source on Long Island that specialized in asset searches. He did all the work, submitted a report, and we transposed it to our letterhead and submitted it to the union. A no-brainer. The union would then put a lien on the deadbeat's account.

Things were going well except for the fact that Willie would vanish for days at a time and would never tell me where he'd gone. When I would ask him where he'd been for the last three days, he would change the subject or give me a vague answer. Now, anytime you're doing work that involves unions there is always a distinct possibility that you might be under the scrutiny of some branch of the Justice Department. An aura of suspicion always permeated union politics and the game of "Wire, Wire, Who's Wearing the Wire" was always a popular pastime at union gatherings. I was concerned that Willie might have been compromised.

Finally, I cornered him one day. We were in our office and I sat on his desk. He was behind it.

"Okay, no pussyfooting," I said. "I tried to call you for the last two days. I also tried your beeper. Nothing. What's up?"

Willie looked like he was about to give me the dog-ate-my-homework type of excuse again, but he knew I wouldn't take a vague answer. "I moved in with Alice," he said sheepishly.

"Alice who?" Fat Alice immediately came to mind but I dismissed it as absurd. Willie was a single guy who always had a beautiful woman with him. The girls loved the Mr. Universe body and Willie was a fun guy.

"Fat Alice." He grinned stupidly.

"What! That pig! What are you, fucking brain damaged?" I couldn't believe it. Suddenly I was glad we weren't legal partners. This guy had to be unstable.

The thought of a naked Fat Alice made me physically sick. Was he actually having sex with the behemoth?

"Listen, man, that broad is gonna make me rich." He told me that after Fat Alice quit her job she had instituted a sexual harassment suit against the Teamsters. She was scared that some union tough guy might hurt her, so she had contacted Willie. She couldn't pay him, but she promised him big bucks after she won the lawsuit if Willie would guard her. Willie saw dollar signs: Fat Alice was suing for millions of Twinkies—I mean dollars. He figured, why not really cement the deal? So he gave up his place on Staten Island and moved, bag and baggage, into Fat Alice's Brooklyn Heights apartment.

Willie's personal life was none of my concern, but I saw potential danger here. A few weeks back I had decided to take a peek at Willie's billing just to see what kind of profit he was making. I found no bills, reports, or any correspondence between W. G. Brandon and the carpenters. In any operation where a union was involved it was wise to keep records pertaining to union activity out of file cabinets and computers because all the material could be subpoenaed in the event of an investigation. Now I wondered where the records were.

"They're in Fat Alice's apartment. Don't worry, they're safe," he said, convinced that they *actually were* safe.

I shook my head. Who knows what he'd told her about what went on at the secret meetings he attended? "You're nuts. I hope you know what you're doing." It still didn't explain to me why he wasn't available for days at a time. I figured maybe he got pinned under Fat Alice and I let it go.

We continued the collections. I got my salary every

week, but the money we had located from the dead-beat contractors was well into the seven-figure area. Willie was getting rich billing the union for hours we worked. But I was happy with my end. Still, I kept thinking about what Willie had told me about keeping his company records in Fat Alice's apartment. I had a nagging feeling that Fat Alice was going to be Willie's yellow taxi.

Fat Alice was as big as a taxi, but that's not what I'm talking about. My friend the Vietnam veteran who volunteered for Vietnam because he "wanted to blow shit up" once told me a story that I'll never forget. He had been assigned to the airborne school at Fort Benning, Georgia, when the war was in its infancy. In those days, the army's policy for informing the relatives of soldiers killed in Vietnam was to dispatch a cab from a local taxi company with a driver clutching a telegram telling them that their loved one had been killed in action. Whenever a yellow cab was spotted cruising through the residential streets of Fort Benning, the whole community would be gripped by fear. In front of whose home was the yellow taxi going to stop?

Fat Alice was going to be Willie's yellow taxi. She would strike the death knell for Willie and the entire union, I was sure of it. I only hoped that I wouldn't go down with them. Guilt by association was a favorite government ploy. The RICO statute was written with unions and organized crime in mind.

About two weeks after Willie's revelation, I spotted cars following me. From the time I left my house until I returned, I had company. Initially, I thought the Russians were making a move. I couldn't trust them to keep their word to leave me alone and I was always cautious. But after the tail continued for a week I knew that if it was the Russians, they would already have taken their shot. They had plenty of opportunity to kill me early in the morning or late at night. I also eliminated the police. They didn't have the resources to mount this type of investigation unless they were tracking a serial killer. No, these guys had to be federal agents.

I hadn't seen Willie in a few days. Now I actively sought him out to warn him about the surveillance. If they were following me, they almost certainly were following him, but I didn't think he had the street smarts to spot them. Willie might have been able to teach me a thing or two about how to survive on Riker's Island, but he didn't know the street. Willie was nowhere to be found. After trying several gyms, I even called Fat Alice. No answer.

The following morning I left for work as usual. I had driven a few miles when two unmarked cars sandwiched me in on a residential street just as I was about to get on the Staten Island Expressway. Four men in suits bounded from the cars. I didn't see any guns, but I instinctively reached for my nine millimeter. I suddenly realized I would be facing off with federal agents. No Russians I knew shopped at Brooks Brothers.

They were polite enough but wanted to relieve me of my weapon. I was happy to comply. I was searched but not cuffed. The guy doing the frisking identified the four as FBI agents. They let me park my car. I rode with them to Foley Square, in Manhattan.

At the FBI's downtown office I was questioned for four hours on the business practices of W. G. Brandon and the carpenters. They wanted to know about the spending habits of Freddy Devine and John Abbatemarco. I stuck with my I'm-only-an-employee story because it was true. I told them about the collections.

"Do I have a problem here?" I asked, definitely concerned.

One of the agents shook his head. "Just a routine investigation. I wouldn't worry about it. Go back to work."

No one seemed overly concerned at the union either. It was business as usual. Willie surfaced the next day like nothing had happened. I told him about my episode with the FBI agents.

"Not to worry, man. You work in unions long enough, you'll be on a first-name basis with every FBI agent in New York." He shrugged. "I've been questioned a few times over the years. They come on like gangbusters, come flying out of cars . . . try to scare the shit out of you. It's all crap. They had anything, Freddy'd be in the can. Relax."

I relaxed. We continued to do our collections, asset checks, and a little bodyguard work. With Abbadaba gone, I was rarely called upon to attend meetings and the daily routine became tedious. But tedious was beginning to look good. I was home every night; my wife liked that, and normalcy began to creep back into my life.

One Sunday night I was parked in front of my television set when the telephone rang. It was Frankie Black. I didn't know whether to be elated, disappointed, or concerned.

"Frankie," I said, "long time. How've you been?" I

tried to keep it light, hoping he was calling to chew the linguine or whatever mobsters do. No such luck.

"Not bad, Wags. Club's coming along, not the same without you." He cleared his throat. "Listen, pal, I need a favor."

My self-destructmobile went into overdrive.

chapter fourteen

I was early for my meeting with Frankie. Very early. Between mad Russians, FBI agents, a partner whom I couldn't locate half the time, and my nagging foreboding about Fat Alice, I was more than a little paranoid.

I was sitting with my back to a wall in a small Italian restaurant on 104th Street, off Broadway, waiting for Frankie Black to show up. I toyed with a menu and wondered why wiseguys always picked Italian restaurants to hold meetings. If they wanted less scrutiny, they should have had sit-downs in libraries. For all I knew, I was under video surveillance. I smiled and waved for the hidden camera. The couple at the next table looked at me and quickly averted their gaze. Their eyes said it all: another crazy New Yorker.

Frankie was ten minutes late. The owner, an old Italian with a practiced accent, greeted him with the usual cheek kisses. They spoke to each other briefly in their language, the old man genuinely happy to see

231

Frankie. Frankie must get a check in this place, I thought.

Frankie spotted me from across the room and gestured to a table by the kitchen. It was a race to the seat facing the door—Frankie won. He pinched the crease on the pants of his black gabardine suit, shot his cuffs, and slid into the leather seat.

"You're looking good, Wags," he said, eyeing my silk shirt, apparently pleased that I wasn't wearing a jacket. No jacket, probably no wire.

I may have looked okay but I felt like shit. My nerves were frayed in anticipation of what Frankie's "favor" might be. I didn't know if I would be leaving the restaurant with the burden of having to hijack a truck, murder someone, or drive Frankie to Saratoga for the racing season. I wasn't hungry but I knew I'd be forced to eat something. Mob guys never conduct business on empty stomachs nor do they trust people who don't have hearty appetites.

"I'm happy," I said. "The union's got me doing day work, it's conducive to a normal lifestyle. My family likes that."

We had drinks, discussed the merits of family life over whore-mongering, and ordered dinner. The small talk and eating before discussing business is also part of the ritual. If I hadn't been so damn nervous about our dessert conversation I would actually have enjoyed myself. Over espresso and the best cannoli I ever had Frankie finally got down to business.

"I really appreciate you meeting me like this," he said. "I know they keep you busy over there."

Like I had a choice. "Always time for you, Frankie." I sipped my tar-colored coffee.

"I've got a little problem I need you to help me with." He reached into his pocket and extracted two Cubans. I don't smoke them, but I wanted something to do with my hands. Cigarettes don't require much in the way of histrionics. We went through the standard cigar-lighting ceremony. I hoped my slight tremble wasn't noticeable.

"There's some guys in Queens owe me money. Not much, a coupla Gs. They pay me every few weeks. I've got two Mooks doing the pickups, but they're new and I don't entirely trust them." His head was enveloped in smoke; a red lampshade behind him cast him in a devilish glow. "I want you to make the pickups with them for a few weeks, report back to me that they're doing okay and not stealing from me. You can do that?"

"Gee, Frankie, I don't know," I said, knowing damn well that the "owed" money was probably gambling debts. "The union wouldn't be too happy with me taking a month—"

"Three weeks," he interrupted.

"Three weeks, even, off. Nah, they wouldn't go for it."

He raised a well-manicured hand. "It's been taken care of. I made a call. You're off for the next three weeks. You'll help me out here?"

What choice did I have? I owed him my life and he was trying to make it look like I had an option. What I could do was to lay some ground rules and see if he'd go along with them. "First, who am I working with? Second, no rough stuff, you're not hiring my gun. Agreed?"

He didn't say anything for a few seconds as his eyes bored into mine. I didn't think he was used to someone else making the rules. After what seemed like an eternity, he blinked. "Two guys, Lenny and Nathan. Like I said, they're new. They work on the door at a club in Queens. Collecting will be a little new to them, but I told them no rough stuff. They get outta hand, that's what you're there for, but it ain't gonna happen. I already laid down the law. The guys you'll be picking up from, we been doing business with for years. They'll hand over the money no problem."

"Three weeks and I'm off the hook?" As soon as I said it I realized I had made a poor choice in phrasing.

He pulled back, feigning shock. "Wags, 'off the hook'? This is a favor. No one's forcing you to help me." He tapped an inch-long ash into a glass ashtray. "But I'll tell you what . . . I don't think I'll be needing any more favors from you after this."

Of course, looking back on the request I know I should have turned him down. What was he going to do, have me shot? I think I knew Frankie well enough to know that refusing this particular favor wasn't a capital offense but I wasn't thinking clearly. The worst that could have happened was that maybe I'd be blackballed from working certain security jobs. But I wanted to get rid of my obligation to him and get on with my life. I felt I could control the situation. Then there was that feeling of invincibility and my quest for another thrill. Three weeks, what could possibly go wrong that I couldn't handle?

"Okay, I'll do it."

"Good, I really appreciate it." Frankie produced an index card from his pocket. "These are the two guys you'll be working with. I gave 'em your beeper number. They're working at the club that's on the card. Meet them there tomorrow night, anytime after nine.

You go from there. Call me at the number on the card every night when you're done. Watch what you say on the phone." He looked around for a waiter and got a check. "Oh, yeah, the money's the same."

"What money?"

"What you were getting paid by the union. I'll be matching it." He grabbed my forearm and grinned. "Don't sweat it. Three weeks, I'll know if these guys are worth keeping on, you get back to the union."

Sure.

The next night I drove to a run-down topless club in Corona. There was one guy on the door. I introduced myself.

"You Lenny or Nathan?" He was six-two and had to weigh at least two hundred and seventy-five pounds. If that wasn't imposing enough, he was wearing biker garb: soiled jeans, black leather vest, and faded T-shirt. The imposing part was the Mohawk haircut. His face looked like it had seen a few knife fights, with him being the loser. This was one ugly dude.

"I'm Lenny," he said, eyeing me. "What the fuck's a Wags?" He had the predatory stare of someone who has done some serious time.

"Frankie Black—"

"Oh, yeah." Too much marijuana had destroyed brain cells. He looked over his shoulder. "Nathan's inside. Come with me." As I followed him, he reached into his pocket. "I got a list of places we gotta hit. Here." There were three addresses on the paper.

"Whose car we taking?" I asked. Lenny gave me a blank look.

"Got no car, me or Nathan." Great, now I was a chauffeur.

We went down two flights to a dingy basement. The second half of the human late notice turned out to be a little less scary. He was slightly shorter than me, with close-cropped brown hair and a droopy mustache. He was wearing the same biker uniform and had the identical jailhouse glare. "I'm Nathan," he said, making no move to shake hands. He was seated on a plastic chair, eyes glued to a television, watching a Scooby Doo cartoon. Two intellectuals.

"Wags," I said, wishing the night over. I decided to play with him a little. "You a big cartoon fan?"

He nodded dumbly, eyes still on the TV. "Not much else to do in the joint."

"I got a videotape of Scooby Doo outtakes. You know, mistakes Scooby made before a final take. Want it?"

Now he looked at me, eyes blinking, a vacuous expression on a face that betrayed no emotion. "Yeah, man, sure."

We went upstairs. I waited for Lenny to tell his boss he and Nathan were leaving for the night. I directed Lenny and Squiggy—my new names for them, from *Laverne & Shirley*—into the backseat of my car. The rear end lowered noticeably. Before I pulled out I wanted to get some things straight. I looked at them in the rearview mirror.

"First, a few things. Either of you guys armed?"

A few seconds of dead air. "Huh?" Lenny said.

"Guns. You guys got jammies?"

"No guns," they said in unison. Both produced switchblades that opened with sharp twangs. "We got these," Squiggy said.

I turned around, draping my arm over the seat.

"Hand 'em over." They hesitated for a second, then complied.

It took us five minutes to get to our first destination, a private house located next to Flushing Meadow Park. I knocked. A short Hispanic man came to the door. Lenny said, "Envelope?" The man handed over a thick legal-size envelope without saying a word, then slammed the door. One down. The next two stops proved to be just as simple; private homes, occupants ready with money.

I dropped the mental giants off at a train station, drove home, and called Frankie.

"Problems?" he asked.

"Nope. Three stops," I said.

"Thanks." He hung up.

I figured that if this was all I was going to have to do for three weeks it was an easy way to pay back a favor. The next night proved to be a little different.

I picked up Lenny and Squiggy at the topless club. Lenny handed me a piece of paper with four addresses on it. "What are these," I asked, "private homes?"

"Massage parlors," Squiggy said, smirking.

They were all located within five blocks of each other in the Woodside section of Queens. Predominantly an Irish residential area, Woodside had one major commercial strip along Roosevelt Avenue under the elevated Flushing IRT train, now called the Orient Express because the last ten years had seen an influx of Asians. The area under the train was known for its whorehouses and gambling dens.

The first massage parlor was located behind a Chinese restaurant. We were admitted quickly enough. The lone Chinese guy on the door didn't ask who we were or what we wanted. He probably thought we were just three white guys looking for some Chinese fortune nookie. The room beyond the double-locked door was dark and smelled of stale beer.

A makeshift plywood bar stood perched on two police barriers to our left. There was a very pretty Chinese woman pouring beer for several Asian male customers. Seven more Asians sat on chairs scattered around the room. Everyone was smoking. There was a big metal bell suspended from the ceiling, next to the bar. Three women—young girls, actually—were giggling and joking with three of the seated men. When we went in everyone stopped what they were doing and stared at us. I stood by the door while Lenny walked up to the bartender. Lenny said a rehearsed "Envelope."

The barmaid looked toward the back and hollered something in Chinese. While we waited for something to happen, I asked Squiggy, "What's the bell for?"

"They ring it every half hour. Tells the broads in the back time's up."

A slight Asian came from behind a curtain and approached Lenny, who was now draped over the bar trying to grab the barmaid's ass. As the man and Lenny began to talk, Squiggy drifted away from me and started talking to a Chinese girl who couldn't have been more than sixteen. I watched them disappear behind the same curtain the Chinese guy had used. Ten minutes passed. All of a sudden Lenny's subdued conversation ceased and he erupted with a huge bellow. Conversation in the room stopped.

I was frozen, anticipating what would come next. In a split second Lenny grabbed the Chinese man by the lapels and rammed his face against the bell. A resounding gong reverberated through the small room as the little man fell to the floor in a heap. Squiggy came tripping from behind the curtain, stuffing his shirt into unfastened trousers.

I rushed over to the unconscious Chinese man on the floor. He was bleeding heavily from the mouth. Lenny leaned over the bar and with two gargantuan arms lifted the entire cash register into the air. He tossed it like a toy onto the grimy floor. Money spilled everywhere. I jumped on Lenny, grasping him in a bear hug. It was like embracing a giant redwood. "What the hell are you doing?" I said. He shrugged me off. He was breathing heavily, eyes hooded, head bobbing and weaving. "Motherfucker won't pay." He went for the prostrate Chinese, arms wide in anticipation of tearing him apart. I stood between him and his victim. Over my shoulder I detected seven frozen Asians. No one was moving. Three more girls came from behind the curtain. The poor bastard on the floor began to groan. He propped himself up on an elbow and said something in Chinese. The barmaid came from behind the bar.

"No more," she said, waving frantically. "I get you money."

She disappeared behind the curtain. Squiggy followed her. Within three minutes she came back with a pile of bills in her hand.

"You take," she said, fear in her eyes. Lenny snatched the cash in a big paw. He had calmed down. I began backing toward the door. Lenny and Squiggy sauntered out like nothing had happened.

We piled into my car. I drove a block before I turned on my headlights. "I said no rough stuff, asshole!" I was pissed. The two brain surgeons ignored me.

"Where the fuck were you!" Lenny screamed at Squiggy.

A dejected Squiggy spoke softly. "I was in the back, Lenny, getting my dick sucked. I figured you could handle it."

"Hey, what the fuck," Lenny said, "you're supposed to back me up, dickhead. What happens if that fuckin' gook had a piece? I'd be fuckin' dead."

"Who was that fuckin' slope, anyway?" Squiggy said. "I never seen him before."

Maybe not, I thought, but his face rings a bell. I pulled the car over underneath the Brooklyn-Queens Expressway.

"What're we stopping for?" Squiggy asked. "We got a coupla more places."

I turned to face them. "We haven't got shit. Get outta the fucking car." We got into a staring contest.

"Hey, man," Lenny said, "we're in the middle of fuckin' nowhere."

"Out!" I screamed. They got out.

I went through three red lights trying to find a pay phone. I was steaming. I misdialed twice before I got Frankie Black's number right.

"Frankie, Wags. We got a problem."

"I know, I know. Our friend just called. What'd you do, drop them off in Jersey?" He sounded amused.

"This isn't funny, Frankie. You promised no rough stuff. I know I owe you, but I'm out. I can't afford to be around nutcases like these." My heart was pounding. If I was going to have my first big one, now was the time.

He tried to calm me down. "Take it easy. That's what you're there for, to control them. Believe me, it won't happen again."

"I got another two weeks plus of this? No way." I didn't care if he handed me over to the Russians on a platter.

"Look, just do the week, okay, then you're out of it."

That mollified me. "Okay, but if either of these psychos raises a hand to another one of your so-called clients, I'm gone."

"Deal," he said, then hung up.

The following night I pulled up in front of the topless club and honked. This time Squiggy was out front and disappeared inside to retrieve his demented buddy. They didn't mention the previous night and I chose not to either.

"Where to?" I asked, hoping to keep the conversation to a minimum. A beefy hand clutching a piece of paper extended over the seat. "Here," one of them said.

There were six addresses listed, three that we'd missed the night before plus three new ones. The first five pickups went smoothly. All were Asian gambling dens or whorehouses. Someone was waiting with an envelope in each one. By the time we got to the last stop it was a little after two in the morning.

This massage parlor was located in the basement of a six-story residential building in Elmhurst. It was posher than the others, with a real bar you could actually belly up to without fear that it would collapse under the weight of a glass of beer. The lighting was soft, with red light fixtures—how appropriate—dotting the walls. Tables were minuscule but clean. There were some Asian types present, but the crowd was predominantly Hispanic, all male. Most were dressed in suits and loosened ties and could have been businessmen who had stopped for drinks and some fast blow jobs before heading home. Either that or they were heavily armed drug dealers unable to sleep after sampling their own product. I hoped it was the former. There were two women behind the bar, serving the boisterous customers. Several scantily clad Hispanic women floated through the crowd getting their tits grabbed. In all, a cohesive group.

Lenny asked for someone named Tony. Tony, one gorgeous barmaid explained, had left for the night. Even Lenny, not exactly a nuclear physicist, figured this to be a logical excuse, given the late hour, so we left.

The next night was more of the same. I'd seen more prostitutes in three days than a sailor on shore leave in Hong Kong, but at least things were going smoothly. Lenny need only extend his hand to get the required envelope. I had begun to relax and reported to Frankie every night that his collection team seemed up to the daunting task of picking up money. The last stop, once again, was the massage parlor in Elmhurst. This time we got there before midnight and Tony was nowhere to be found. Again we left, but Lenny and Squiggy grumbled about "lack of respect."

Tony was MIA for the next three trips. Finally, on the sixth visit, Lenny and Squiggy went into a huddle with a Hispanic guy who said he was Tony's cousin. I stood with my back to the door. The joint was crowded, with about twenty drunks jammed into a space that could have comfortably fit fifteen. But by this time we had become familiar faces, so no one really paid much attention to us. That is, until Lenny tossed a chair into the bottles of cheap booze behind the bar.

"Listen up, you spic motherfuckers!" he hollered as he squeezed Tony's cousin's head in a viselike head-lock. "This scumbag's cousin owes me money"—he scanned the crowd, psycho eyes daring anyone to dispute his words—"and since he ain't never here, you cocksuckers are gonna pay it for him!"

I was making a move for Lenny—Squiggy had gotten swallowed up in the crowd somewhere—when I saw a young Hispanic kid—who couldn't have been more than eighteen reach ever so slowly beneath a windbreaker.

Now I had a choice: Go for Lenny and break up the clinch he was in with the poor schmuck he had in the headlock or deal with a potential gunman. I chose to survive.

I was carrying a revolver in an ankle holster. I raised my leg, removed the pistol, and let it dangle by my side, finger off the trigger. The kid who was making his move thought better of it and removed his hand from his jacket. At the same time, Squiggy emerged from the crowd.

"Toss your wallets onto the floor," he said. He was unarmed, but had his right hand in his coat pocket. Slowly, customers began to comply. Wallets hit the carpeted floor silently.

I had had enough. I hadn't signed on to be a party to this. Screw these guys and Frankie Black, too, I thought. "I'm leaving," I said. I began to back toward the door, holstering my gun as I moved.

Lenny turned to me sharply, jerking his prisoner like a rag doll. I thought he was going to snap his neck. "Where the fuck you goin'?"

I said the first thing that came to mind: "I need a smoke. I'll be outside." He just stared at me and grunted. Squiggy was too busy retrieving wallets to notice my departure.

I left the building and walked slowly toward my car, calmly lighting a cigarette. I didn't know if either of the two mental giants was behind me and I didn't want to turn around to find out. My car was parked just around the corner from the basement entrance. As soon as I made the turn, I sprinted to my car. I was out of there quicker than a guy caught by a jealous husband.

I woke up the next morning to a beeping pager. My wife had already departed for work and I showered and put on a pot of coffee before answering the page. The call was from a highly pissed-off Lenny.

"Where the fuck did you take off to? Me and Nathan came outside and you was gone."

"That's because I left, stupid. Listen," I said, "you and I are severing our relationship. You and your buddy are jerkoffs. I want nothing to do with you." I hung up and did my best to forget about Lenny and Squiggy.

Around noon I called the number Frankie had given me. He answered after fifteen rings.

"Yeah," he said groggily.

"Wags, Frankie. There was another to-do last night, Lenny tell you?" I heard some grunts.

"Yeah, yeah. He called me all pissed off. What happened? How come you didn't call me?"

"Because," I said. "I quit. Those mamalukes started lifting wallets from the customers in Tony's club. I want no part of it. I'm out."

Frankie sighed. "Yeah, yeah, okay. I'll talk to them. It's okay, you're out, I understand. I'll be in touch." He hung up.

I figured I had closed the last chapter on Frankie Black. I went back to work at the carpenters' union. Everything seemed like it was back to normal—or in my case, abnormal. There were still rumors of an FBI investigation into the union, but no one seemed unduly concerned. I settled back into my routine.

A few weeks later I got another page from Lenny. I let him dangle for a few hours before returning the call.

"I got pinched," he said.

"Pinched? For what?" Why the hell was he calling me? None of this was my problem, but I was curious and let him talk.

Lenny and Squiggy couldn't leave well enough alone. They kept going back to Tony's club looking for him. They were not only collecting what he owed them but they were shaking him down for thousands more. They figured Tony would never go to the police, seeing as how he was running a whorehouse and gambling den. Surprise.

"He went to the One-Ten Precinct and reported us," Lenny said. "They wired the prick and he gave us marked money. We got busted. We're out on a hundred G's bond."

"Gee," I said. "I'm all teary-eyed. That's what you get for breaking the law. I gotta go."

"Not yet you don't. I need seventy-five hundred."

"From who?"

"From you . . . to pay my lawyer or I'm going to tell the cops you was with us the first time and maybe a few others. Look, I ain't gonna talk about this on the phone." He gave me a street corner in Howard Beach. "Be there tomorrow at noon."

The following day I showed up at our meeting place at nine-thirty A.M. If Lenny was setting me up for an ambush, I wanted to be there before the shooters got in place. I waited in my car, smoking, until he showed up, right on time. He was the passenger in a late-model Cadillac driven by a washed-out-looking blond woman. He spotted me and motioned me to the Caddy. The blonde left the two of us alone in the front seat. After she walked away I spotted her writing down my license-plate number.

We talked for almost an hour. He still wanted $7,500 for his lawyer. My feeling was that if I gave him the money, it might not be the last time he would hit me up. I also didn't know if he hadn't already given me up. He could have told the police anything. It's not rare for someone caught holding the bag to give up a cop, or an ex-cop. Prosecuting a former cop, particularly a sergeant and one with my record, would have been a plus for any prosecutor's career. I felt I hadn't done anything I couldn't talk my way out of. I had drawn my gun to protect myself and had left the club shortly thereafter. While I shouldn't have gotten involved in the first place, I felt my involvement wasn't something I could be arrested for. I began formulating a plan that would get me off the hook completely.

"Let me think about it for a while," I said as I left the car. "Call me in a few days."

"Well, don't take too long makin' up your mind. I gotta go back to court in a week. If I have to do a bit, you're goin' down with me."

I called Frankie Black when I got home. He had gotten me into this mess and I counted on him for getting me out of it. The conversation lasted all of five seconds.

The instant he heard my voice he said, "Don't call me anymore," and hung up.

During the course of the next week, Lenny called me three times. Each conversation was recorded. I got him on tape trying to shake me down. At the same time I got him to go over my actual involvement during the incident at Tony's place. If he was going to testify that I was an active participant in a shake-down attempt, I now had the taped evidence to refute it. Once I had what I considered to be enough taped evidence, I told Lenny not to call me again; I wasn't going to give him the money. He made threats. I hung up on him.

I took the tape and my story to my attorney, George DiLeo. George thought I had good evidence to show the police that while I might not have used good judgment in taking Frankie Black's job, I wasn't guilty of extortion.

After listening to the tape a few times, he got up from behind his desk. "Okay, let's go," he said.

"Where to?"

"You're turning yourself in. Sort of a preemptive strike before Lenny turns you in and invents all kinds of ridiculous shit to save his ass." It sounded like a good idea at the time, but it turned out to be a disaster.

The 110th Precinct detective assigned to the case took us to the Queens racket squad in the DA's office. A platoon of ADAs listened to the tapes and my explanation for getting involved with Lenny and Squiggy in the first place. Afterwards George and I waited in an outer office for what seemed an eternity. Finally, one of the ADAs emerged. "Hang loose," I was told, "you'll be contacted if anything comes of this."

Three months passed. I was back full-time at the union. As time crept by my initial fear of getting arrested diminished. My lawyer was confident that my problem had blown over. I heard that Lenny and Squiggy were going to trial. There was no mention of my name.

Late one Tuesday evening my phone rang. It was my attorney.

"We got a problem." He sounded ominous.

My heart sank. "What?"

"You've got to surrender tomorrow at the One-Ten. You're getting arrested."

I could be the world's best writer and not be able to fully convey the multitude of emotions that coursed through my body when I heard those words. Fear: jail time for a former cop. If I survived I'd be a broken shell of what I once had been when, and if, I got out. Shame: How do I tell my family? If the story made the papers—and New York newspapers love ex-cops-who-get-locked-up stories—I knew my kids would be humiliated in school. And what of the reputation I had built over the years? What would become of my business, my PI license, my future? Anger: I had done nothing criminally wrong. What had Lenny and Squiggy said about me to save their own asses?

I felt my insides heaving; my head was swimming. "What the hell happened?" I asked my lawyer. My mouth was dry; the words came out garbled.

"The Queens DA thinks you put Lenny up to taking all the heat. He thinks the tapes were rehearsed, that you paid Lenny to get you out of it. To the DA's way of thinking, Lenny's going to jail anyway, and you probably paid him to take the blame."

I couldn't believe what I was hearing. "You going to be there with me?"

"I played a trump card, Wags. I tried to postpone the arrest till I had a chance to work on getting you out of it. I told the DA's office I'd be out of town. Didn't work. They want you at the One-Ten tomorrow at nine o'clock to turn yourself in. Now I can't go, they think I'm in Florida or wherever the hell I told them I was going. I'll send another lawyer. Try not to worry, I'll have you out on bail, fast."

"What's the charge?" I asked, hoping for a misdemeanor. I heard George swallow.

"Robbery, twenty-one counts, one for each of the patrons the night you were in the joint and pulled your gun."

"Jesus, George, I didn't rob—"

"Wags, I know that and you know that, but you're a former cop, a sergeant, no less. You're a career maker for some ambitious DA. Besides, you and I know charges don't mean shit. They'll be dropped or reduced. Don't worry."

"What if they don't drop them, what kind of time am I looking at here?" My voice squeaked, the emotion and fight taken out.

"Wags, don't worry, don't—"

"George, what am I lookin' at!?" I yelled. It took all the energy I had.

There was a moment of silence. "Life."

The rest of the conversation was a blur. I recall my mind racing and nausea approaching. I hung up and waited for my wife to come home

The rest of the day I spent curled up on my bed in

the fetal position. It's times like these when cops kill themselves. Criminologists call it "the availability of the gun." If there was ever an excuse for ending it all, it was then. Don't think it didn't cross my mind. What saved me from a foolish act was my family. I love my wife and children more than my own life. No matter how much torture I was about to be subjected to, I knew I could survive because while I might lose almost everything, including my freedom, I would still have my family. No matter what I was branded, my family would still love me. No matter what.

I broke the news to Pat as soon as she came home. Pat's always been a tender, loving person, particularly good with our children. That day I saw her tough side. We'd make it together, she said. We'd survive as a family. After considerable thought we decided not to tell the kids until it was over. My son was no longer ill, but could stress cause a relapse? The girls were still very young. I would wind up keeping the arrest a secret for the entire legal process, about six months. My kids are sharp, but they never suspected anything. Now you know why some cops choose acting as a second career. I think every cop needs to be a good actor in order to survive. I gave an academy-award performance for months. I thank God the story never made the papers.

I decided I would surrender alone. This took some doing because Pat wanted to be there with me. I didn't want her to see me in cuffs. I couldn't bear the shame or the pain I would be putting her through. I would go it alone.

* * *

The next morning I dressed in boots (no laces) and jeans (no belt). I took just the money I would need for tolls and a little pocket change. Personal items and anything I could use to take my own life would be taken away from me. I didn't want to give my keepers that satisfaction.

I drove to the 110th Precinct in a fog, like I was on automatic pilot. After circling the street a few times, I parked a block away from the station house, threw my car keys under the driver's mat, and went to face my future.

The detective who handled the original investigation, Detective Terry Troise, filled out the myriad paperwork required for any arrest. She was courteous, but ill at ease. I don't think she wanted to be locking up an ex-cop. She was doing her job, no matter how distasteful. Her boss, some pompous lieutenant, glared at me every chance he got. I kept quiet, just answering statistical questions, offering no excuses or opinions. Nothing I could say now, I thought, would have any bearing on the outcome of the case. I was comforted in knowing I'd be in my own home that night, the long ordeal before me on the horizon.

After processing I was cuffed, an indignity I protested to no avail, and driven to central booking, located in the basement of Queens Criminal Court. Once there, I was photoed and given a private cell. Hours passed. I began to get apprehensive. Where was my lawyer? Why hadn't I been released on bail?

The cell began to fill up. I was now sharing my space with five lowlifes who would have loved to know their cell mate was a former NYPD sergeant. I wouldn't have survived the night.

Somewhere around midnight I was tossed a bologna

sandwich and some lukewarm Kool-Aid. I didn't dare sleep. A favorite topic of conversation in holding cells is comparing charges. One grungy character who was tossed in the cell in his underwear asked me what I was in for.

"I ripped the 'Do-Not-Remove-Under-Penalty-of-Law' tag off my sofa," I said. "Cops broke down my door and locked me up. Fucking ex-wife turned me in."

"They bust you for that?" he asked, wide-eyed.

"I'm here, ain't I?"

In the morning some cop took pity on me and told me that my paperwork had gotten "lost." Paperwork tends to get lost when someone wants the prisoner in question to suffer by keeping him in the can longer than required. It can take literally days to find "lost" paperwork. I was able to catch the ear of a sympathetic cop who promised to look into "the problem."

Still no lawyer. I had now been incarcerated about eighteen hours. I would find out later that my attorney's request to have another lawyer represent me had been ignored, or simply forgotten by his colleague. I wound up with legal aid for the arraignment. After twenty hours in jail, I was finally released on my own recognizance for a future court date. Finally, the first step was over.

Since I had been arrested for a felony, a grand jury would have to indict me in order for the process to move forward. The state had 180 days to secure the indictment. After that time, if there was no indictment, charges would have to be dismissed. The clock started to tick. Every day I went to work at the union like nothing had happened. Time passed—ten days, fifty days, a hundred and thirty days. My lawyer called me and told me he'd heard the DA was waiting for me to talk.

"Talk about what?"

"They want to know who was behind the collections. They know it wasn't you, and Lenny and Nathan haven't got the smarts. You tell them who asked you to get involved, testify against him, and you'll probably walk, or at least take a small hit."

All my life I've believed in the philosophy of keeping my mouth shut. It was ingrained in me as a kid by my peers, carried over into the navy and the New York City Police Department. It's a way of life for someone who has to survive on the streets of New York. You don't rat out, no matter what the price. I was socialized to conform to that doctrine. I was comfortable with it. Too many people try to rationalize their behavior by blaming someone else for their actions. I dug my own hole, made my own choices. I didn't feel it was right to drag anyone else down with me, Frankie Black included.

"There's no one to turn in, George." I'd take my chances with a jury or a plea bargain.

A few months into my ordeal, I was called into a union leader's office. The union had heard about my arrest, and he wanted the particulars. I gave him the facts, leaving nothing out. I was surprised when he said the union was behind me, that I had been loyal to them and now they were going to be loyal to me. I still had my job.

One hundred and seventy-eight days. No indictment. Had I called the DA's bluff? Did they have enough to indict me? I had no idea what Lenny and Squiggy had told the DA or if they had been believed.

In two more days I would be a free man.

Then I got the call. It was my lawyer.

"Wags," he said, weariness in his voice, "you've been indicted."

epilogue

I hung tough to the very end. The Queens DA still wanted me to implicate the person who had been pushing the buttons. I still refused to tell them anything. The DA was incensed that I wouldn't cooperate and recommended a felony plea bargain rather than the misdemeanor it should have been. With little choice other than to talk, I accepted the plea.

If I had given up Frankie Black, I would be in the witness protection program living somewhere in Minnesota eating pizza that tastes like cardboard. My family would have been uprooted, and I'd be looking over my shoulder for the rest of life. This, plus the guilt I'd carry to the grave with me for betraying my own rules.

I left the courtroom on the day of my sentencing with mixed emotions. On the one hand, happy that I was a free man, I looked forward to getting home to my family. On the other hand, I was gripped by the fear that my problems would begin all over again with the new subpoena I still had clutched in a sweaty hand.

Apparently, rumors that the carpenters' union was under some sort of federal investigation had proved correct. But what could I contribute to the investigation? Was I a witness or a target of the grand-jury probe? I resisted an impulse to get to a phone and call the office. Federal investigations meant phone taps. I didn't want my voice saved for posterity.

I spent a celebratory evening at home with my family. Pat and I finally sat the kids down and told them what had transpired during the last six months. Jimmy, my oldest, was a little peeved that he hadn't been privy to my problems from the beginning, but was happy to know his dad wouldn't be a number in an upstate condominium.

I was still anxious about the union. After three unanswered phone calls to Willie Gonzalez, I gave up and resigned myself to waiting to find out what was going on until the next day, when I would go to work. I felt relieved knowing that I at least still had a job. The union's troubles were their own. I went to bed that night silently praying that I was only going to be a witness in the grand-jury probe. I tried to relive in my mind the time I'd spent with the union. Was there something in my day-to-day duties that could be construed by the feds as illegal?

The office was in total chaos when I arrived early the next morning. There were two armed security men guarding the front door who at first refused me entrance but relented when I identified myself as retired from The Job. About twenty men in business attire who were unfamiliar to me were changing locks and keeping Freddy's people out of the office. Amid the confusion were several secretaries who were in tears.

My head was swimming. There wasn't one union official present who could tell me what the hell was going on. In the midst of the turmoil I spotted Beau Dietl. I hadn't had any contact with him in years. When he saw me, his eyes bugged.

"What the hell are you doing here?" he asked.

"I work here," I said sheepishly.

He shook his head. "Not anymore, buddy." He explained that he had been hired by the International Brotherhood of Carpenters in Washington, D.C., to shut down and secure the New York office after the grand-jury probe had been announced. He was coordinating a raid that would make Jimmy Doolittle proud.

Freddy Devine was indicted, along with other union officials for misappropriation of union funds. He pleaded not guilty. John Abbatemarco was not indicted. Vendors, Beau told me, such as leasing companies, the people who owned the corporate jet, limo operators, and other companies that did business with the union had received subpoenas.

I was out of a job. I considered asking Beau for work—I had always been impressed by his thoroughness and professionalism—but knew that my days as a security specialist were more than likely over. I left the office that day depressed anew, worried about what fate awaited me from the grand jury and how I would support my family.

Accompanied by my attorney, I testified before the federal grand jury a few weeks later. The lag time gave me the opportunity to find out what had happened to kick off the indictments and the dismantling of the New York office.

Fat Alice had brought the union down. Not much of a surprise. What did surprise me was Willie's role in the case.

It was alleged that while Willie was working with his former partner, they had been conducting a secret investigation for the union. They were supposedly hired to get dirt on a federal judge named Kenneth Conboy. Conboy had been appointed as an overseer of the union. In that capacity he was investigating the spending practices of union officials. Fearing what he might find, certain union bosses allegedly hired Willie and his partner to follow the judge, hoping to find evidence of strange sexual predilections in order to blackmail him.

While Willie was conducting that investigation, Fat Alice got the word that she had lost her sexual harassment case. Willie, knowing his meal ticket had just expired, dumped Fat Alice quicker than you could say "Hey, is that a Twinkie you have there?" Fat Alice, the hippo scorned, took all Willie's case folders, including notes on the Conboy investigation, and turned them over to the feds.

As of this writing, the federal investigation into the carpenters' union is still continuing. Willie Gonzalez literally vanished off the face of the earth. Rumor has it that he's either dead, the victim of someone's ire, or is residing somewhere in America under the cloak of the witness protection program, waiting to testify at someone's criminal trial. Willie may be pumping iron in a gym near you even as you read this. Lenny and Squiggy are in prison doing three years and eighteen months, respectively. Topsey's is still open. McReady has been replaced by another mob-appointed figurehead.

As for me, my PI career ended with my conviction. I voluntarily gave up my private investigator's license, figuring it would probably have been pulled anyway. I didn't need a license to do security consulting, however, or to work under someone else's license. Career hopes were also dashed after I testified before the grand jury. Even though I testified only as a witness (I had little to say but to describe my daily duties), the word had gotten out in a paranoid industry that I had testified. In the hush-hush world I had inhabited, testifying was akin to a Klansman celebrating Kwanza. It just wasn't done. Any talking that is preceded by the words "I do" is a career destroyer. My career, which had been circling the drain for months, now had its final gurgle.

Despite the fact that I had to take out a twenty-thousand-dollar second mortgage on my home to pay for my defense, and I am starting my post-NYPD life all over again, I still consider myself lucky. My wife and kids—the ones in *public* school—don't care whether I'm rich or poor, just as long as I'm around. They'll be seeing a lot of me in the near future. I've given up the pager, the cell phone, and the fast life. Now if people need me, I'm on the Internet at wags@dp.net. My son is teaching me the wonderful world of the Internet.

I've recently accepted a new assignment as the director of security for the Witkoff Group, a real estate investment company. Steven C. Witkoff, a forty-one-year-old attorney, is the president of the company. He's a genuinely nice guy who owns over eleven million square feet of prime Manhattan commercial real estate. As with guarding any wealthy, powerful person, the threat of violence, kidnapping or other crimes is always there, but being immersed in the fast-paced word of New York real estate is a far cry from the world with which I had become familiar. I'm learning a lot from a man who negotiates $100-million deals without so much as a pen or a calculator; he has made me a member of his corporate family. I thank Steve Witkoff for providing me with a second chance.

I look back often at the whirlwind life I led and the people whose paths I crossed—Willie Gonzalez, who, if he's still alive, will be hiding for the rest of his life; Hondo, who is still risking his neck hustling for a buck, alone and sharpening his knives; Beau Dietl, who is undoubtedly planning his next raid into a Third World country even as we speak; and the countless others who have corrupted their values to make the extra dollar or experience the next thrill.

I wish all of them luck.